The BIG Book of
CREATIVITY
GAMES

Other books in *The Big Book of Business Games* series:

The Big Book of Business Games
The Big Book of Customer Service Training Games
The Big Book of Flip Charts
The Big Book of Humorous Training Games
The Big Book of Motivation Games (by Robert Epstein & Jessica Rogers)
The Big Book of Presentation Games
The Big Book of Sales Games
The Big Book of Stress-Relief Games (by Robert Epstein)
The Big Book of Team Building Games

The BIG Book of

CREATIVITY

GAMES

Quick, Fun Activities for Jumpstarting Innovation

Robert Epstein, Ph.D.

Editor-in-Chief, *Psychology Today*
University Research Professor, United States International University
Director Emeritus, Cambridge Center for Behavioral Studies
Chairman and CEO, InnoGen International

McGraw-Hill

New York San Fransicso Washington, D.C. Auckland Bogotá
Caracas Lisbon London Madrid Mexico City Milan
Montreal New Delhi San Juan Singapore
Sydney Tokyo Toronto

McGraw-Hill

*A Division of The **McGraw·Hill** Companies*

1 2 3 4 5 6 7 8 9 0 AGM / AGM 0 9 8 7 6 5 4 3 2 1 0

ISBN 0-07-136176-6

The sponsoring editor for this book was Richard Narramore, the editing supervisor was Paul R. Sobel, and the production supervisor was Charles Annis. This book was set in Arial by Jessica Rogers. Printed and bound by QuebecorWorld / Martinsburg.

McGraw-Hill books are available at special quantity discounts to use as premiums and sales promotions, or for use in corporate training programs. For more information, please write to the Director of Special Sales, McGraw-Hill, 2 Penn Plaza, New York, NY 10121-2298. Or contact your local bookstore.

This book is printed on recycled, acid-free paper containing a minimum of 50% recycled de-inked fiber.

To Julian, Justin, Jordan, and
a brand-new baby girl, as yet unnamed–
my four greatest creations.

CONTENTS

ACKNOWLEDGMENTS

I'm grateful to my editor at McGraw-Hill, Richard Narramore, for guiding me through every step in the conception and preparation of this volume. These games would not exist without the many students with whom I've had the privilege of working over the past 20 years, both in my laboratory and in the classroom. You helped me to develop the scientific theory that underlies these games, as well as to refine the games for classroom use, and for that, I'm grateful. In recent years, many fine people in the business community have given me the opportunity to refine the games for the business audience. Carol Marturano-Becker and Dr. Lyle M. Spencer, Jr. have been especially helpful. Jessica Rogers, an editorial intern at *Psychology Today* and a student at the University of California Berkeley, has provided invaluable assistance in the preparation of this manuscript. Thanks, yet again, Jessica!

The BIG Book of

CREATIVITY

GAMES

getting
ready...

THE NEW SCIENCE AND TECHNOLOGY OF CREATIVITY

These aren't just any old games. They're games born of extensive laboratory research on the creative process. So before we starting fooling around, let's take a quick look at the underlying science.

Myth Busting

Everybody knows that creativity–the ability to express ideas which are both new and valuable–is mysterious, right? And even a 6-year-old can tell you that creativity is located in the right brain.

But systematic research on the creative process in individuals shows otherwise. In fact, many common conceptions about creativity prove to be shaky when you look at the creative process carefully.

> *Myth: Creativity is rare.* Actually, research shows that the neural processes that underlie creativity are universal. We couldn't make our way through a new shopping mall or say a new sentence without them. Creative *expression* is rare, but that has more to do with the way we're socialized than it does with ability. In fact, we all probably have the creative potential of Mozart, Einstein, and Picasso. Want to know how to tap that potential? Keep reading!

> *Myth: Only high IQs have creativity.* Several studies reveal a correlation between intelligence and creativity, but correlational studies don't shed light on causal relationships. In other words, no study has ever shown that any particular degree of

intelligence is *necessary* for creativity, and there are plenty of prominent artists, inventors, poets, and composers of average smarts.

Myth: Creativity can't be studied. The first psychology laboratory was established in the late 1800s. Before that, many people claimed that human thinking and behavior would forever be beyond the reach of scientific understanding. But learning, memory, development, and many other aspects of human behavior are now studied routinely in laboratories around the world, and enormous advances have been made on every front. Research on creativity began in the 1950s, with careful laboratory studies beginning in the 1970s. And, again, enormous advances have been made.

Myth: It's in your right brain. Studies of a small number of split-brain patients in the 1960s stimulated a Left-Brain-Right-Brain craze that has gotten completely out of hand. Keep in mind that there are only a few dozen people on the planet whose brains have been surgically split; the other five billion of us have intact brains, the two halves of which are joined by perhaps 100 million nerve fibers. No one has ever found a specific neural location for creativity, and people who claim to be able to train you to use a dormant side of your brain are deluding you, themselves, or both.

Myth: Creativity is mysterious. Actually, some important aspects of the creative process in individuals are now well understood. The process will probably always *feel* mysterious because feelings of frustration and confusion often accompany the process. But some of the basic laws that govern the generation of new ideas have now been discovered, and significant practical applications of the basic science are well underway.

Myth: Creativity can't be learned. In fact, virtually everyone can learn to express greater creativity. The key is to develop some simple skills or "competencies," which are as easy to learn as, say, tying your shoes. Exercises in this book will help you master these skills, and the last chapter will even allow you to test your current skill levels.

If you want to talk to a group about the myths that surround creativity, you might want to make a handout or overhead transparency from the figure on page 10. Figures suitable for copying are included throughout this book.

Generativity Theory and Research

The games in this volume are based on a body of scientific research called "generativity" research, which focuses on understanding the emergence of novel behavior continuously in time. In the early 1980s, this research yielded a formal scientific theory called Generativity Theory. Expressed as a series of equations and various computer models, the theory has shown that novel behavior in individuals–the kind of behavior that is sometimes labeled "creative"–is orderly and predictable. In the laboratory, novel behavior can even be predicted moment-to-moment in time.

The basic idea behind Generativity Theory isn't new (ironic, isn't it?). People suggested long ago that new ideas come from combinations of old ones. Generativity Theory simply expresses that concept more precisely. Generativity research also demonstrates how certain types of experiences influence the creative process. For example, the research shows that there is an orderly relationship between what we have learned and the new ideas we can express, and it also shows that failure (or "extinction") helps spur the creative process in predictable ways. For a more detailed look at Generativity Theory and research, consult other books by the author, or read about the theory in the new *Encyclopedia of Creativity,* published by Academic Press.

The figure on page 11 summarizes the basic features of Generativity Theory, and the figures on pages 12 and 13 summarize the practical implications of the theory. Again, you might find it helpful to make overheads of these figures for group activities.

Just How Competent Are You?

Generativity research pinpoints four "core competencies"–underlying skills and tendencies–that help people express their creativity. Remember that *everyone* has roughly equal creative potential. People who express creativity frequently have mastered certain core skills, and anyone can master these skills:

> *Capturing.* New ideas are often fleeting. They come, they go, they're gone, like a rabbit scurrying through the woods. "Creative" people have learned to preserve new ideas as they occur–to preserve first and evaluate later. Fortunately, it's easy to learn ways to capture new ideas, and strengthening skills in this competency area alone will often boost creative "output" by a factor of 10 or more.

> *Challenging.* Failure sets in motion a behavioral process called "resurgence"–the reappearance of old behaviors that used to work in situations like the current one. If you have trouble turning a door knob, for example, you'll quickly resort to methods that used to work on other doors: turning harder,

kicking the door, shouting for help, even shouting for your mom. The good thing about this process is that it gets multiple behaviors competing with each other, and when behaviors compete, new behaviors are often born. In other words, failure spurs creativity. The bad thing about this process is the way it feels: Behavioral competition feels confusing or frustrating. This competency area involves a variety of techniques for managing failure–for eliminating the fear of failure, for seeking and limiting failure, and for managing the emotions that accompany failure.

Broadening. If you're writing your first symphony, and you've never heard any music other than symphonies by Beethoven, your style will probably be limited. The more diverse your existing "repertoires of behavior," the more interesting and diverse the interconnections. Therefore, one of the simplest ways to boost creativity is to broaden your knowledge base. In other words, instead of taking another course on Windows architecture, try one on Medieval architecture.

Surrounding. Multiple behaviors are also set in motion by multiple or unusual stimuli in the environment. Imagine approaching a stop light, for example, on which both the red and green lights are illuminated. How would this very unusual (and very broken) stimulus make you feel and behave? Your right foot will probably tap dance between the accelerator pedal and the brake pedal, during which time you'll feel somewhat confused or uncertain (great emotions when it comes to creativity). The point is that we can accelerate and direct the creative process by managing our environment systematically–both the physical environment (the decorations in our office, for example) and the social environment (the people with whom we work and play).

A variety of research also suggests that managers, teachers, parents, and other supervisors need some special competencies–eight in all–in order to elicit creativity in other people. This book contains games that teach and strengthen all of the four core competencies–the main focus of the book–as well as all of the eight managerial competencies. The figures on pages 14, 15, and 16 summarize the individual and managerial competencies.

In addition to the basic competency areas, it's often important to provide people with some basic creativity training. This is helpful because the misconceptions about creativity are so strong. Most people believe they're not creative, for one thing; some simple games will quickly convince them otherwise. The next chapter will show you how to use the 48 games in this book for basic creativity training, for strengthening specific competencies, and for common organizational purposes.

A competencies approach has been enormously helpful in improving leadership, sales, and other abilities. Generally speaking, training people produces far greater economic benefits–and far fewer lawsuits–than "selecting" people. It also avoids the hazards of labeling. Nothing in this book should lead you to label someone "creative" or "dull." Since research shows that generative processes are universal, all of the games in this book focus on building skills and knowledge–all of which lead to greater creative expression. No labels, please.

Okay, Let's Fool Around

Just as the competencies approach has been helpful for managing human resources, the games approach has been a breath of fresh air for training. Games are as engaging for adults as they are for kids, and that's the point:

8

Properly constructed games make learning fun.

Many of the games in this book were developed for college students–and then revised and refined with business executives–with two purposes in mind: to *teach* about the creative process, and to *boost and direct* creative expression. Their dual purpose makes them fairly unique in the world of creativity training. The idea is not just to boost creativity but also to teach basic principles that will help people boost their own creativity throughout their lives.

Want More?

Some of the games in this book are described in more detail in Epstein's *Creativity Games for Trainers*, published by McGraw-Hill in 1996. For further information about Generativity Theory, check *Cognition, Creativity, and Behavior,* published by Praeger in 1996, or, as noted above, consult the new *Encyclopedia of Creativity*. For more information about creativity training and testing, contact InnoGen International at www.innogen.com or 1-877-INNOGEN. To contact the author directly–preferably with praise and money–write repstein@post.harvard.edu.

MYTHS ABOUT CREATIVITY

It's rare.

Only high IQs have it.

It's in your right brain.

It can't be studied.

It's mysterious.

GENERATIVITY BASICS

➢ Competing behaviors produce new behaviors.

➢ The combinatorial process is orderly and predictable.

➢ By influencing the type and number of competing behaviors, we can accelerate and direct creativity.

IMPLICATIONS OF GENERATIVITY THEORY

➡ Everyone has roughly equal creative potential.

➡ "Creative" people have special skills.

➡ Anyone can learn these skills.

➡ The creative process can be accelerated and directed.

LESSONS FROM GENERATIVITY RESEARCH

- ❢ People need to learn to *pay attention to* and to *preserve* their new ideas.

- ❢ *Failure is invaluable* for creativity, because it causes ideas to compete.

- ❢ *Broad training* is important for creativity, because it makes diverse ideas available to compete.

- ❢ Properly-designed *physical and social environments* can stimulate creativity by causing ideas to compete.

Four Core Competencies For Individual Creativity

CAPTURING
Preserves New Ideas

CHALLENGING
Seeks Challenges and Manages Failure

BROADENING
Broadens Skills and Knowledge

SURROUNDING
Changes Physical and Social Environment

CREATIVITY COMPETENCY DEVELOPMENT

❶ CAPTURING
Carrying notebooks, tape recorders
Finding the right place and time
The Three B's: Bed, Bath, and Bus
Daydreaming and sleep
The hypnogogic state
Anonymous channels

❷ CHALLENGING
Controlled failure systems
Open-ended problems
Ultimate problems

❸ BROADENING
Sign up for training in new fields.
Read, listen, and learn outside your area of expertise.
Spend a day a month in a "foreign territory."

❹ SURROUNDING
Relocating
Redecorating
Scheduled changes
Cross-functional teams
New magazine, newspaper, journal subscriptions
Intelligent screen savers

Managers, Teachers, Supervisors: Eight Competencies

1 Encourages the Preservation of New Ideas

2 Challenges Others

3 Encourages Broadening of Knowledge and Skills

4 Manages Surroundings to Stimulate Creativity

5 Manages Teams to Stimulate Creativity

6 Manages Resources to Stimulate Creativity

7 Provides Feedback and Recognition to Stimulate Creativity

8 Models Appropriate Creativity-Management Skills

HOW TO USE THIS BOOK

This chapter will help you decide which games are best suited for your needs. Find your purpose, and the pertinent game titles will follow. The games themselves follow this chapter in alphabetical order by title, so you'll find them easy to locate whether you're just starting out or already familiar with the games.

Each game chapter begins with a thumbnail sketch of the game, followed by sections that will tell you how much time you'll need to play the game, what people will learn from the game, what supplies you'll need, and how to run the game. Discussion questions follow, along with suggestions for customizing the game for different settings and situations.

The book also includes several "Design Challenges," in which participants are asked to design their own games, along with various "Workplace Challenges," in which participants are asked to apply what they've learned to their particular workplaces.

What's Your Game?

Why do you want to play creativity games? Some common purposes are listed below, along with the titles of the games that you'll probably find most helpful for accomplishing your goal. If you don't find your purpose in the list, try the "competencies" section later in this chapter. If that doesn't work, start flipping pages until you see titles, phrases, or art that catches your eye. (Alternatively, use the classic "blind" strategy: Close your eyes, flip through the book, and stop at some random page. Check out whatever game you've come to; it's probably good for *something*. This is a "surrounding" technique, by the way–great for spurring creativity.)

Note that the same game might be helpful in more than one category.

Purpose: <u>*Convincing people that they're creative*</u>
Games: Capturing a Daydream (p. 73)
Selling a Zork (p. 163)
The Srtcdjgjklered Game (p. 171)
The Tell-Me-a-Story Game (p. 191)

Purpose: <u>*Getting a project off the ground*</u>
Games: The Amazing Magazine Game (p. 33)
The Anonymous Suggestion Game (p. 35)
Bridges to Creativity (p. 45)
Broadening: *Workplace Challenge* (p. 57)
Capturing: *Workplace Challenge* (p. 71)
Challenging: *Workplace Challenge* (p. 81)
Creative Potential: *Workplace Challenge* (p. 87)
The Experts Game (p. 89)
The Lola Cola Game (p. 109)
Managing Resources: *Workplace Challenge* (p. 117)
Managing Teams: *Workplace Challenge* (p. 123)
The Memory Game (p. 127)
The Monkey-Do Game (p. 131)
The Odd Couple Game (p. 149)
The Popsicology Game (p. 153)
The Shifting Game (p. 167)
Sticky Business (p. 177)
Surrounding: *Workplace Challenge* (p. 185)
The Ultimate Challenge Game (p. 203)
The Ultimate Design Game (p. 207)

The Memory Game (p. 127)
The Lola Cola Game (p. 109)
The Ultimate Challenge Game (p. 203)
The Experts Game (p. 89)
The Odd Couple Game (p. 149)
The Srtcdjgjklered Game (p. 171)
The Tell-Me-a-Story Game (p. 191)
What D'Ya Know? (p. 213)

Purpose: <u>*Two-day seminar (in suggested order)*</u>
Games: Capturing a Daydream (p. 73)
Selling a Zork (p. 163)

Building a Better Capturing Machine (p. 63)
The Memory Game (p. 127)
The Random Doodles Game (p. 157)
The Anonymous Suggestion Game (p. 35)
Capturing: *Workplace Challenge* (p. 71)

The Lola Cola Game (p. 109)
The Not-for-the-Fainthearted Game (p. 145)
The Keys to Creativity (Basic and Advanced
     Versions) (pp. 99, 105)
The Ultimate Challenge Game (p. 203)
Challenging: *Workplace Challenge* (p. 81)

The Experts Game (p. 89)
The Broader the Better (p. 59)
The Amazing Magazine Game (p. 33)
The Odd Couple Game (p. 149)
Broadening: *Workplace Challenge* (p. 57)

21

Focus on Competencies

If your main interest is in boosting creativity in a particular setting–say, to rescue a failing organization or to keep a business competitive–you might want to use the games to build specific creativity competencies. In this case, start your session by administering the test in "What D'Ya Know?" (page 213), and choose games that will strengthen the kinds of skills that people need most. This test is an abridged version of the *Epstein Creativity Competencies Inventory for Individuals* (*ECCI-i*), which measures the four core competencies that underlie individual creativity. The *Epstein Creativity Competencies Inventory for Managers* (*ECCI-m*), which measures the eight competencies that are important for the management of creativity in other people, is not included in this volume.

Here is a list of the twelve competency areas, along with games that can help you build those competencies:

CORE Competency 1
Preserves New Ideas (Capturing)
Games: Building a Better Capturing Machine (p. 63)

And with that, as some highly-placed ancient Romans used to say (more or less), "Let the creativity games begin!"

the
games!

THE ABCs OF CREATIVITY

In a Nutshell

The group leader asks some volunteers to spell a series of words using children's alphabet blocks. Some volunteers are given a series of easy tasks before being given a difficult one; others start out with a difficult task.

Time

30 minutes.

What You'll Learn

Success can interfere with your creativity and your ability to solve problems. If you've been too successful in some situation, you may be insensitive to changing conditions.

What You'll Need

A set of standard children's alphabet blocks, and a timer or clock.

Before conducting this game, you must prepare the alphabet blocks. The preparation is simple, but you must do it carefully, or the game will fail. All you need to do is to remove all blocks containing the letter "T" (both uppercase or lowercase). That's easy enough, but when you remove those blocks, you will also be removing other alphabet letters–the ones on the blocks with the Ts on them. When you do that, you may need to modify the list of words that you will be asking the first group of volunteers to spell (see next page). The participants should be able to spell these words using letters on the blocks.

What to Do

Part One: Select six volunteers, have one sit at the table in front of the room, and send the other five out of the room. You may also wish to select someone to serve as the official timekeeper for the game. The timekeeper is stationed at the table in front of the room. The timekeeper should be equipped with a stopwatch or timer and with a bucket of alphabet blocks.

Now, ask the timekeeper to dump the blocks. Ask your volunteer to spell BOX–as quickly as possible. As soon as the volunteer has located the correct alphabet letters and arranged them in order (this should only take a few seconds), congratulate the volunteer, and have the timekeeper announce the time and record it. This procedure should be repeated for the words ZIP, MAN, HOP, and LIT.

The volunteer should have no trouble with the first four words (BOX, ZIP, MAN, and HOP) but may have some difficulty with LIT, because the blocks do not contain any Ts. The solution is simple, of course—if you're a child! You simply use any blocks to form the shape of a T, or perhaps the shapes of all three letters (L, I, and T). In any case, the solution time for LIT will probably be longer than for the first four words.

Part Two: Now the fourth, fifth, and sixth volunteers should be given their chance; however, they will be asked to spell just one word: LIT. The instructions from Part One of the game should be modified accordingly.

When all six of the volunteers have completed the task, the timekeeper needs to compute only two numbers: the average time it took the first group (of three volunteers) to spell LIT, and the average time it took the second group to spell LIT.

Typically, the average time is much longer in the first group than in the second. Previous success at solving the problem a certain way interferes with creativity when the problem changes.

Discussion Questions

1. Was everyone able to spell LIT? Did some people have more trouble than others? Who had trouble, and why?
2. Did experience on the simple spelling tasks help or hurt on the more difficult task?
3. Previous success can both help and hurt when you're faced with a new problem. Can you think of examples?

Alternative

Change the words to suit your needs, but do so cautiously. It's important that all of the words be the same length, and all of the words except the test word should be easy to spell using the alphabet letters printed on the blocks.

If You're Short on Time

You may want to cut down on the number of volunteers. Instead of three volunteers for each part, try just one volunteer for Part One, and another for Part Two. You can even skip Part Two altogether and still get your point across.

Tip!

Some people may get frustrated when they can't find the letter T. Remember that in the context of these games, frustration is a good sign, not a bad one. Reminding the group that that's the case will relieve some of the pressure. Feel free to offer encouragement. The phrase, "You can do it!" can work wonders.

THE AMAZING MAGAZINE GAME

In a Nutshell

Participants are asked to develop as many new products as possible using certain magazines.

Time

20 minutes.

What You'll Learn

Diverse stimuli enhance creativity.

What You'll Need

Six magazines for every pair of teams: Three magazines from a particular business or industry, and three colorful popular magazines, each very different from the other (e.g., *Vogue, Psychology Today,* and *TV Guide*).

What to Do

Divide the group in two, with the Rockin' Readers on one side of the room and the Super Subscribers on the other. Divide each subgroup into teams of about five people. Now give each Rockin' Reader team three serious trade magazines, and give each Super Subscriber team three colorful popular magazines. Next, give the teams 15 minutes to develop as many new products and services as possible, using the magazines to help them. The Super Subscribers should outperform the Rockin' Readers. Lead a discussion about the results.

Discussion Questions

1. Which team developed the most ideas? Why?
2. What effect did the colorful popular magazines have in the creation of new ideas?
3. How could the results of this game be applied to your workplace?

Alternative

Instead of asking the participants to create new services or products, give them a naming task. For example, have them think of new car or cola names. For added drama, wrap all of the magazine in brown paper before you distribute them, and have people unwrap them when you give the signal to begin.

THE ANONYMOUS SUGGESTION GAME

In a Nutshell

Participants make suggestions for solving a sensitive societal problem—either with or without the protection of anonymity.

Time

15 to 20 minutes.

What You'll Learn

People are usually more willing to express their creative ideas when they can do so anonymously—that is, when the risk of ridicule or punishment is removed.

What You'll Need

You'll need to create two different survey forms—those that protect anonymity and those that don't. You may want to use copies of the forms on pages 38 and 39.

What to Do

Distribute Form 1 (page 38) to half the group and Form 2 (page 39) to the other half. Explain that you're going to be comparing the types of suggestions people make when they must reveal their identities to the types of suggestions they make when they can remain anonymous. (In fact, that's not exactly what this game is about. We'll get to that in a minute.)

Have people list suggestions for reducing crime on our nation's streets. You can propose a different task if you like. Make it relevant to your particular group.

When the forms have been completed, explain that you're not actually interested in comparing the types of suggestions that have been made but rather the *number* of suggestions. Do people make more suggestions–especially on sensitive topics– when their identities are secret?

Have a volunteer collect the forms and compile a quick tally of the number of suggestions made by members of each half of the group. If the group is typical, people in the anonymous half will have made many more suggestions (on the average) than people in the half without anonymity. (In a small group, outlying values can unfairly skew the mean; the more appropriate statistic is the median.)

Lead a discussion about how these results can be applied to improve suggestion systems in the participants' work environments. What is the ideal suggestion system for encouraging people to express their creative ideas on a regular basis? (See "Tips!" that follow for suggestions.)

Discussion Questions

1.   Do people respond differently when their anonymity is assured? How so?
2.   Even assuming that people are more honest or creative when they can remain anonymous, a suggestion system that does not allow people to claim their good ideas would surely fail. Why?
3.   What's wrong with a suggestion system that requires people to identify themselves?
4.   Why are people often reluctant to contribute their ideas to the group?

Tips!

In the workplace, you can boost creative expression by establishing a suggestion system that promotes capturing: an anonymous suggestion system that allows people to claim their ideas later. How you set this up—with two-part numbered suggestion forms, with special email addresses and codes, with a bulletin board system—depends on your particular work environment.

Remember, a new idea is like a gold brick falling from the sky: Everyone wants to catch it, but no one wants to be crushed by it. And all but a few think that it's probably fool's gold, anyway.

Survey (Form 1)
The Anonymous Suggestion Game

Your name (required):_____ Telephone (required):__

Other contact information:_____

Please list your suggestions below:_____

1.

2.

3.

4.

5.

6.

7.

8.

9.

10.

Survey (Form 2)
The Anonymous Suggestion Game

Please list your suggestions below: _____

1.

2.

3.

4.

5.

6.

7.

8.

9.

10.

THE AUDIENCE GAME

In a Nutshell

Some volunteers perform a naming task while facing the audience, and others perform the same task while facing away from the audience.

Time

15 minutes.

What You'll Learn

People are rich sources of stimuli. To enhance your creativity, you should surround yourself with interesting and diverse physical and social stimuli—and that includes people.

What You'll Need

You'll need six chairs that you can move around in front of the room, as well as writing materials for your volunteers.

What to Do

Select six volunteers and seat three of them so that they face the audience and the other three so that they face away from the audience. If space allows, place the latter three people so that they can't see each other, either. Give writing materials to all of the volunteers.

Now ask all of the volunteers to list as many new hairstyles as they possibly can in 10 minutes. Everyone has heard of hairstyles like "crew cut," "shag," and "afro." How many new hairstyles can people invent? For each hairstyle, people should write a name for that style, along with a very brief description of the style, or a sketch of that style. Have the volunteers raise their hands high for a moment whenever they add a new style to their lists.

For added drama, have a scorekeeper keep a simple tally on a blackboard or flipchart. The tally should show the number of times people raise their hands in each of the two groups—Audience and No-Audience.

When the time is up, inform the audience of the total count in each of the two groups, elicit some examples of new names from each group, and lead a discussion about the results. The Audience group will normally produce more new names than the No-Audience group, because it's easier to invent new hairstyles when you have a variety of real hairstyles to examine. In other words, new ideas come more easily when you have access to diverse, relevant stimuli.

Discussion Questions

1. Did the two groups (Audience and No-Audience) produce different results? What were the results, and why did they differ?
2. Did the individuals in the two groups behave in a noticeably different way during the task? How so?
3. Social stimuli would normally inhibit performance on a task like this. Why?
4. In a group or team situation in which everyone can participate, social stimuli are often inhibiting. Why would that normally not be the case in the task we just completed?

If You Have More Time

You might try increasing the work period to 15 minutes. Longer time periods should accentuate the difference between the groups.

Alternatives

For a smaller group, you might try using just four or even two volunteers. Instead of having volunteers raise their hand, you might want to have them ring a small bell every time they add a new idea to their list.

BRIDGES TO CREATIVITY

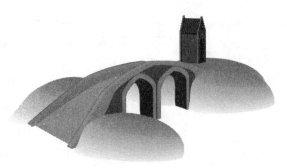

In a Nutshell

Two teams build bridges
using foam blocks, having first been given slightly different
instructions.

Time

20 minutes.

What You'll Learn

Sometimes very subtle differences in instructions can make
a huge difference in creativity. In this game, participants
learn the importance of "open-ended instructions" in a team
activity.

What You'll Need

You'll need a bucket of 50 lightweight foam blocks, sold
commercially under the name "Tub Blocks." You'll also need
two sheets of white legal-size paper, a marker, and a ruler.
Two small tables, spaced well apart, should be set up in front
of the room. Make one copy of the instructions on page 51,
and cut the sheet in half where indicated. The top half will go

to the Crafty Constructors (Team 1) and the bottom half to the Bodacious Builders (Team 2).

The Tub Blocks, all of which are about 1-inch thick, come in a variety of shapes. You'll need to create two identical sets of blocks, one for each team. In each set, you might want to include the following blocks:

(2)	6-inch by 1.5-inch rectangles
(4)	3.5-inch by 1.5-inch rectangles
(4)	3-inch by 1.5-inch rectangles
(1)	3-inch square
(2)	triangles
(2)	half-circles
(2)	circles

It isn't critical that you use exactly these blocks or that you use this particular brand. Before you begin the game, however, be sure that you practice building bridges with whatever materials you've decided to employ.

On the sheets of paper, mark two parallel lines, 10 inches apart, as shown at the top of the following page. The space between the lines will be the "river" in the game.

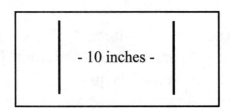

- 10 inches -

What to Do

Before displaying the materials, appoint two teams–the Crafty Constructors and the Bodacious Builders–with three people in each, and send them out of the room. Appoint a timekeeper.

Now explain to the group that you'll shortly be asking each team to build a series of bridges that span a river. Set up a diagram on each table, and pour the blocks next to each diagram. Explain that you'll be giving slightly different instructions to each team. The Crafty Constructors (Team 1) will get typical, everyday instructions–the kind that imply a limit:

> *Your task is to use the provided building blocks to span a river, marked by two parallel lines on the sheet of paper on the table. In your final structure, no blocks may touch the space between the two lines. You have a maximum of 10 minutes in which to complete this task.*

The Bodacious Builders (Team 2) will get superior instructions, called "open-ended" instructions, the kind that explicitly say that the solution is unbounded in one or more respects.

> *Your task is to use the provided building blocks to build the <u>widest possible bridge</u> that you can. At a minimum, it must span a river, marked by two parallel lines on the sheet of paper on the table. In your final*

structure, no blocks may touch the space between the two lines. You have a maximum of 10 minutes in which to complete this task.

Even though the teams have exactly the same resources, will the open-ended instructions produce superior performance? Will the Bodacious Builders build wider, more creative, more interesting structures than the Crafty Constructors?

Bring the teams back into the room, station them at their respective tables, and give them their written instructions (see page 51). Because it's important that each team not know about the other team's instructions, you mustn't read the instructions aloud, and you won't be able to answer any questions that group members might have. Just get them started, and encourage both teams to keep building until the ten minutes have elapsed.

As soon as one team has completed a structure, use your ruler to get a quick measure of the span of the bridge, and record the measurement on paper. Then knock the bridge down, and ask the team to build another bridge with a different design. Have each team build as many bridges as they can in the allotted time.

Finally, lead a discussion about the effect of open-ended instructions on creative performance. Normally, the Bodacious Builders will build several bridges with spans that exceed the width of the bridge by several inches, whereas the Crafty Constructors will build bridges that are the exact width of the river.

Discussion Questions

1. Did the two teams perform differently? How so?
2. How do open-ended tasks, instructions, goals, and questions differ from conventional ("closed") tasks, instructions, goals, and questions?
3. How do open-ended tasks improve creative performance?
4. What kind of instructions, goals, and tasks are normally given in your workplace? How might open-ended tasks make a difference in both performance and creativity?

Alternative

This game can be done with individuals instead of teams. The main advantage of using teams is to make more hands available to place the blocks and hold the structure steady during the construction process.

Tip!

There are many, many different designs that will span the river, and some that will go well beyond the banks, as the Bodacious Builders will probably demonstrate. A span of 16 inches is even possible. Here's one simple design for a bridge that spans the river. Don't share this with your participants, though. Let creativity rule!

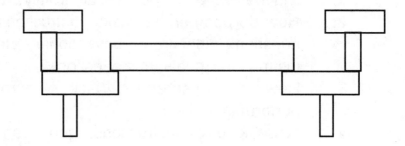

Instructions for the Crafty Constructors

Your task is to use the provided building blocks to span a river, marked by two parallel lines on the sheet of paper on the table. In your final structure, no blocks may touch the space between the two lines. You have a maximum of 10 minutes in which to complete this task.

- ✂

Instructions for the Bodacious Builders

Your task is to use the provided building blocks to build the widest possible bridge that you can. At a minimum, it must span a river, marked by two parallel lines on the sheet of paper on the table. In your final structure, no blocks may touch the space between the two lines. You have a maximum of 10 minutes in which to complete this task.

51

BROADENING:
DESIGN CHALLENGE

In a Nutshell

Participants design and carry out their own exercise to demonstrate the importance of *broadening* (diverse training) in creativity.

Time

Allow at least 40-60 minutes. If you want to have a discussion after the game is complete (see below), plan on about 90 minutes for the whole process.

What You'll Need

The materials will vary with the task that the group designs. Have basic writing materials, a flip chart, and some odd objects on hand. Because "broadening" has to do with training and learning, you might also want to have a variety of different training materials available (see, for example, "The Amazing Magazine Game," page 33).

What to Do

The participants' task is to design and implement at least

one new game that shows how important *broadening skills* are for the creative process. Before you have them take on this challenge, be sure they have participated in at least one similar game, such as "The Experts Game," page 89.

Have people work in small teams, and give them at least 15 minutes in which to design the new game or games. Through a show of hands, see which teams had the most success with their designs, and then select one team to take charge of the whole group and try out one of their new games.

The game should demonstrate one or more of the following lessons: (a) knowledge is essential to creativity, (b) diverse knowledge is especially helpful for the creative process, (c) when knowledge or training is limited in some way, creativity suffers.

After the game is over, lead a brief discussion about what the game may have taught and how it could be improved. Also, find out about some of the other games that had been designed.

If time allows, you can try out another game or two.

Discussion Questions

1. How easy was it to design a new game?
2. What method or methods did you use to get your design team to maximize its creative output?
3. How, if at all, did the game or games you played teach

you about broadening?

4. How might this game be improved to teach people about broadening?

5. What value does diverse training have in the creative process?

Don't Forget!

In a well-designed game, everyone should be able to participate or at least have some fun, and time limits need to be respected. You may want to give the leadership team some tips to help make their game more successful. On the other hand, for extra fun for both you and the group, you might also announce that you're available to *participate* in the team-designed game.

BROADENING:
WORKPLACE CHALLENGE

In a Nutshell

Participants work in teams to develop specific methods for improving *broadening* practices in their workplaces.

Time

20-30 minutes.

What You'll Need

Writing materials, including blank sheets of paper (without lines), for each participant.

What to Do

Divide the group into small teams, and have the teams spend about 15 minutes compiling lists of methods that might enhance broadening skills in their workplaces. If you like, use the "shifting" technique (see page 167) to enhance the creativity of your teams. After the teams are done, have representatives of different teams share their results with the group, and lead a discussion about how to improve broadening in the workplace. If your resources allow, collect the lists, compile them into a master list, and distribute it (by email, perhaps) to all participants.

Discussion Questions

1. Does your organization provide diverse training for its employees?
2. Is your training program optimal for maximizing and directing creativity? How might the program be improved?
3. How might very narrow training stifle the creative process?
4. Providing diverse training can have multiple benefits for an organization. What benefits can you think of?
5. Which of your proposals are most feasible? Which are least feasible? How might you use creative problem-solving techniques to make the latter proposals more feasible?

Don't Forget!

Some of your participants might feel that this is an exercise in futility–that limited resources or shortsighted managers will make it impossible to implement their suggestions. To those individuals you might point out that: (1) stating the suggestion is already a great step forward, (2) resources and managers change from time to time, (3) some suggestions can be implemented at little or no cost, and (4) implementation problems are just more problems to be solved.

THE BROADER
THE BETTER

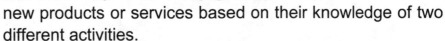

In a Nutshell

First, participants devise new products
or services based on their knowledge
of one activity. Then they generate
new products or services based on their knowledge of two
different activities.

Time

30 minutes.

What You'll Learn

Generally, the more skills—and the more diverse the
skills—that you bring to a problem, the more creative you will
be.

What You'll Need

Writing materials for each participant, and a flipchart or
blackboard.

What to Do

Part One: Ask the participants to give you suggestions for a list of activities they know a lot about. These can be the names of departments or divisions (like Marketing or Sales) or the names of more specific activities (like photocopying or shipping).

Based on suggestions from the group, make a list of between 10 and 20 activities on the blackboard or flipchart.

Now ask people to focus on just *one* of these activities. Based on what they know about it, instruct them to take a few minutes to try to develop one or more new products or services. For example, it can be frustrating waiting in line to use the photocopy machine. Participants could devise a way for people to be entertained while they're waiting–or, better yet, a way for people to get work done. In generating their new ideas, have people try to focus on that one activity only.

Allow people a few minutes to jot down their ideas, and then call on a few people to report their suggestions.

Part Two: Now, inform the participants that you are going to compile a new list–this time, a list of activities that they know about *outside* the organization–activities like singing, mowing the lawn, or bowling.

Based on suggestions from the group, make a new list of between 10 and 20 activities. Once again, be sure these are activities in which your participants have expertise.

Now have people try again to develop one or more new products or services. This time, have them use their expertise in *two* areas—one organizational activity (preferably, the one you used a few minutes ago) and one of the outside activities. So now, perhaps, someone is in the photocopy room again, and this time he or she is also thinking about singing. Perhaps he or she envisions a photocopy machine with a built-in stereo or a built-in kareoke screen. Perhaps then a slight leap is made to a photocopy machine with a running display of today's news or stock market results.

Again, allow a few minutes for people to jot down their ideas, and then call on some of them to report on their new products or services.

Discussion Questions

1. Did it help or hurt to think about two topics at once?
2. If you have problems to solve, are you better off with narrow or diverse training? Why?
3. How could the results of this game be applied to your workplace?
4. How could training in different subject areas be used to direct the creative process?

If You Have More Time

If time allows, you can expand the problem to include two or more outside activities. With more ideas available, you'll probably get more interesting solutions.

BUILDING A
BETTER CAPTURING
MACHINE

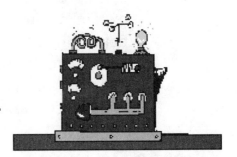

In a Nutshell

Participants are asked to create "capturing machines"–devices that help them preserve new ideas–using whatever materials are at hand.

Time

15 minutes.

What You'll Learn

Ideas are fleeting. To be creative, it's important to preserve new ideas when they occur.

What You'll Need

You have many options here. At one extreme, you can conduct this game with no special materials or supplies, in which case you can ask participants to rely on whatever happens to be at hand. In a barren room, this might not work very well, but it would still be worth doing. You might also want to try a large assortment of bizarre items for this game–anything but a pen and pad! This, too, provides a challenge, and it also makes the game more fun. If you expect to bring two volunteers to the front of the room (see below), then, for dramatic effect, before the game begins you should create two piles of the strange objects and cover each pile with a cloth. Uncover them when you give the "Go" to begin constructing the first device.

What to Do

Describe the task: Working individually, participants will be given 30 seconds to construct a device that they might be able to use to remember a good idea. They'll be able to use anything on hand–including food items, silverware, jewelry, makeup, clothing, and napkins–other than traditional writing implements (pens, pads, pocket computers, and so on). For example, in a pinch, one could use lipstick to jot down an idea on a napkin–or even on one's arm.

Have two volunteers come to the front of the room, and tell them that to construct their capturing devices, they'll have to use the special objects you've provided.

Now signal everyone to begin. After 30 seconds have passed, point out what the volunteers and some other members of the group have built, and have people speculate on how well the device would work. Repeat the procedure until everyone has built (or has tried to build) five devices.

Discussion Questions

1. How difficult is it to create a "capturing machine"?
2. Tell us about an interesting capturing machine that you've created in the past. What idea were you trying to preserve? Were you successful?
3. What did you learn from this game?

Tip!

Your choice of objects for the volunteers is an important factor in determining the success of this game. Modify your collection of objects to make the game as fun and as relevant as possible.

CAPTURING:
DESIGN CHALLENGE

In a Nutshell

Participants design and carry out their own exercise to demonstrate the importance of *capturing* for the creative process.

Time

Allow at least 40-60 minutes. If you want to have a discussion after the game is complete (see below), plan on about 90 minutes for the whole process.

What You'll Need

The materials will vary with the task that the group designs. Have basic writing materials, a flipchart, and some odd objects on hand. For the latter, visit your own garage or attic, or take a trip to the local toy store.

What to Do

The participants' task is to design and implement at least one new game that shows how important *capturing skills* are for the creative process.

Before you have them take on this challenge, be sure they have participated in at least one similar game, such as "The Random Doodles Game," page 157.

Have people work in small teams, and give them at least 15 minutes in which to design the new game or games. Through a show of hands, see which teams had the most success with their designs, and then select one team to take charge of the whole group and try out one of their new games.

The game should demonstrate one or more of the following lessons: (a) that preserving new ideas has value, (b) that *not* preserving new ideas can be costly, (c) that new ideas are fleeting, (d) that it's easy to preserve new ideas, or (e) that it's easier to capture in certain places or at certain times.

After the game has been played, lead a brief discussion about what the game may have taught and how it could be improved. Also, find out about some of the other games that had been designed.

If time allows, you can try out another game or two.

Discussion Questions

1.　How easy was it to design a new game?
2.　What method or methods did you use to get your design team to maximize its creative output?
3.　How, if at all, did the game you played teach you about capturing?

4. How might this game be improved to teach people about capturing?

And Don't Forget!

In a well-designed game, everyone should be able to participate or at least have some fun, and time limits need to be respected. You may want to give the leadership team some tips to help make their game more successful. On the other hand, for extra fun for both you and the group, you might also announce that you're available to *participate* in the team-designed game.

CAPTURING:
WORKPLACE CHALLENGE

In a Nutshell

Participants work in teams to develop specific methods for improving *capturing* practices in their workplaces.

Time

20-30 minutes.

What You'll Need

Writing materials, including blank sheets of paper (without lines), for each participant.

What to Do

Divide the group into small teams, and have the teams spend about 15 minutes compiling lists of methods that might increase the rate at which new ideas are captured in their own workplaces. If you like, use the "shifting" technique (see page 167) to enhance the creativity of your teams.

After the teams are done, have representatives of different teams share their results with the group, and lead a discussion about how to improve capturing in the workplace. If your resources allow, collect the lists, compile them into a master list, and distribute it (by email, perhaps) to all participants.

Discussion Questions

1. How might your workplace be changed to encourage employees to preserve their new ideas?
2. How might your workplace be changed to encourage employees to share their ideas with colleagues and supervisors?
3. How might your organization use incentives, evaluations, computers, anonymous suggestion systems, workspace design, and other means to encourage employees to preserve their new ideas?
4. Which of your proposals are most feasible? Which are least feasible? How might you use creative problem-solving techniques to make the latter proposals more feasible?

And Don't Forget!

Some participants may feel that this is an exercise in futility—that limited resources or shortsighted managers will make it impossible to implement their suggestions. To those individuals you might point out that: (1) stating the suggestion is already a great step forward, (2) resources and managers change from time to time, (3) some suggestions can be implemented at little or no cost, and (4) implementation problems are just more problems to be solved.

CAPTURING
A DAYDREAM

In a Nutshell

Participants are asked to daydream for a few minutes and then to relate to the group the contents of their daydreams.

Time

5-10 minutes.

What You'll Learn

Participants learn that (a) under the right conditions, every one of us has highly imaginative daydreams, and (b) the daydream demonstrates the enormous creative potential we all have.

What You'll Need

No special materials are needed.

What to Do

Explain that you're going to give participants permission to do something they've been forbidden from doing since grade school: permission to *daydream*.

Ask participants to sit in a relaxed position. Have them close their eyes, take a deep breath, and let the breath out slowly. Speak slowly and calmly, and encourage them to relax. Then ask them to let their minds wander freely for a few minutes–perhaps they'll visit other places, see strange images, or hear odd sounds. Perform the exercise with them. Relax and have a daydream.

After 2 or 3 minutes–longer, if the setting permits–ask people to open their eyes and return to reality. Then call on people and ask where they went and what they experienced. How many of them left the room? Did any of them see bizarre images or have impossible experiences? Share your own daydream with the group if the daydream was interesting in some way.

Discussion Questions

1. Where did you go? What did you experience? Did you experience anything odd or fantastic or beautiful in your daydream?
2. Did you have difficulty with this exercise? If so, why? Could the present conditions be the problem? Under what conditions might you be able to perform better than you did here?

3. Were you surprised by how far your daydreams took you? How so?
4. Do you think daydreaming might have any practical value? In what way?
5. How might an artist or inventor use the daydream deliberately for creative purposes? How might you do the same?
6. What stops us from daydreaming more than we do?

Alternative

If appropriate, as soon as you have had the participants open their eyes, have them jot something down about what they just experienced. Daydreams, like night dreams, disappear quickly from memory. Taking notes helps keeps the memory fresh.

CHALLENGING:
DESIGN CHALLENGE

In a Nutshell

Participants design and carry out their own exercise to demonstrate the importance of *challenging* for the creative process.

Time

Allow at least 40-60 minutes. If you want to have a discussion after the game is complete (see below), plan on about 90 minutes for the whole process.

What You'll Need

The materials will vary with the task that the group designs. Have basic writing materials, a flipchart, and some odd objects on hand. For the latter, visit your own garage or attic, or take a trip to the local toy store.

What to Do

The participants' task is to design and implement at least one new game that shows how important *challenging skills* are for the creative process. Before you have them take on this challenge, be sure they have participated in at least one similar game, such as "The ABCs of Creativity," page 29.

Have people work in small teams, and give them at least 15 minutes in which to design the new game or games. Through a show of hands, see which teams had the most success with their designs, and then select one team to take charge of the whole group and try out one of their new games.

The game should demonstrate one or more of the following lessons: (a) that failure can be valuable, (b) that failure can lead to new ideas, (c) that failure should not be feared, (d) that the frustration we feel when we're failing is normal and natural, (e) that open-ended questions and goals are valuable for the creative process, (f) that ultimate questions are valuable for the creative process, or (g) that failure can be controlled and managed.

After the game has been played, lead a brief discussion about what the game may have taught and how it could be improved. Also, find out about some of the other games that had been designed.

If time allows, you can try out another game or two.

Discussion Questions

1. How easy was it to design a new game?
2. What method or methods did you use to get your design team to maximize its creative output?

3. How, if at all, did the game you played teach you about challenging?

4. How might this game be improved to teach people about challenging?

And Don't Forget!

In a well-designed game, everyone should be able to participate or at least have some fun, and time limits need to be respected. You may want to give the leadership team some tips to help make their game more successful. On the other hand, for extra fun for both you and the group, you might also announce that you're available to *participate* in the team-designed game.

CHALLENGING:
WORKPLACE CHALLENGE

In a Nutshell

Participants work in teams to develop specific methods for improving *challenging* practices in their workplaces.

Time

20-30 minutes.

What You'll Need

Writing materials, including blank sheets of paper (without lines), for each participant.

What to Do

Divide the group into small teams, and have the teams spend about 15 minutes compiling lists of methods for managing failure wisely in their workplaces. If you like, use the "shifting" technique (see page 167) to enhance the creativity of your teams.

After the teams are done, have representatives of different

teams share their results with the group, and lead a discussion about how to manage failure in a way that improves workplace creativity. If your resources allow, collect the lists, compile them into a master list, and distribute it (by email, perhaps) to all participants.

Discussion Questions

1. How might your workplace be changed so that employees are regularly challenged in a way that best promotes creativity?

2. How might your workplace be changed so that employees can better manage the stress that accompanies failure?

3. How might your organization structure tasks and goals, conduct meetings, train managers and staff, and use other means to manage and control employee failure?

4. What are the advantages of teaching managers and staff to control and manage failure?

5. What are the risks associated with exposing employees to greater challenges? How can your organization minimize those risks?

CREATIVE POTENTIAL:
DESIGN CHALLENGE

In a Nutshell

Participants design and carry out their own exercise to demonstrate that we all have enormous creative potential.

Time

Allow at least 40-60 minutes. If you want to have a discussion after the game is complete (see below), plan on about 90 minutes for the whole process.

What You'll Need

The materials will vary with the task that the group designs. Have basic writing materials, a flipchart, and some odd objects on hand. The more and the odder the objects, the better.

What to Do

The participants' task is to design and implement at least one new game that demonstrates that we all have enormous creative potential. Before you have them take on this challenge, be sure they have participated in at least one similar game, such as "Capturing a Daydream," page 73.

Have people work in small teams, and give them at least 15 minutes in which to design the new game or games. Through a show of hands, see which teams had the most success with their designs, and then select one team to take charge of the whole group and try out one of their new games.

The game should demonstrate one or more of the following lessons: (a) We all have new ideas throughout the day. (b) Many of our thoughts and images are very strange–perhaps even "artistic." (c) We ignore many of the new ideas that occur to us during the day. (d) We all experience dreams, daydreams, and the "hypnogogic" (semi-sleep) state–potentially enormous sources of creative ideas. (e) In the right setting people can "switch on" a very high degree of creativity. (f) Creative thinking can be facilitated throughout the day. (g) Anyone can write poetry, compose music, paint a picture, or invent something, even if he or she has never done so before.

After the game has been played, lead a brief discussion about what the game may have taught and how it could be improved. Also, find out about some of the other games that had been designed.

If time allows, play another game or two that demonstrates the universality of creativity.

Discussion Questions

1. Are you "creative"? Why or why not?
2. How many people do you believe are creative? How do you know?
3. How many people *might* be able to express creativity? Why might some people currently be suppressing this ability?
4. How easy was it to design your new game?
5. What method or methods did you use to get your design team to maximize its creative output?
6. How, if at all, did the game you played teach you about creative potential?
7. How might this game be improved?

And Don't Forget!

In a well-designed game, everyone should be able to participate or at least have some fun, and time limits need to be respected. You may want to give the leadership team some tips to help make their game more successful. On the other hand, for extra fun for both you and the group, you might also announce that you're available to *participate* in the team-designed game.

CREATIVE POTENTIAL:
WORKPLACE CHALLENGE

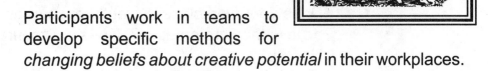

In a Nutshell

Participants work in teams to develop specific methods for *changing beliefs about creative potential* in their workplaces.

Time

20-30 minutes.

What You'll Need

Writing materials, including blank sheets of paper (without lines), for each participant.

What to Do

Divide the group into small teams, and have the teams spend about 15 minutes compiling lists of methods that might teach people in their workplaces about the enormous creative potential they all have. If you like, use the "shifting" technique (see page 167) to enhance the creativity of your teams.

After the teams have finished, have representatives of different teams share their results with the group, and lead a discussion about how to improve workplace awareness about creative potential. If your resources allow, collect the lists, compile them into a master list, and distribute it (by email, perhaps) to all participants.

Discussion Questions

1. Does your workplace currently encourage people to believe they are creative? Does it discourage them? How so?
2. How frequently do people currently express creativity in your workplace? How frequently *might* people be able to express creativity in your workplace?
3. What kind of training might your organization provide to teach people about their creative potential?
4. What other methods might your organization use to teach people about their creative potential?
5. Which of your proposals are most feasible? Which are least feasible? How might you use creative problem-solving techniques to make the latter proposals more feasible?

And Don't Forget!

Some of your participants might feel that limited resources or shortsighted managers will make it impossible to implement their suggestions. You might point out that: (1) stating the suggestion is already a great step forward, (2) resources and managers change from time to time, (3) some suggestions can be implemented at little or no cost, and (4) implementation problems are just more problems to be solved.

THE EXPERTS GAME

In a Nutshell

The leader finds members of the group who are "experts" on esoteric topics, and these individuals teach the group something new about each topic. Based on this knowledge, audience members design a new product or service.

Time

45 minutes.

What You'll Learn

New knowledge, especially in areas well outside one's current expertise, provides important fuel for the creative process.

What You'll Need

Writing materials for each participant, and a flipchart or blackboard.

What to Do

Begin by dividing the group into teams. Next, find a few people on each team who know obscure facts about a special domain such as fishing, sewing, gardening, airplanes, bowling, religion, or politics.

Have these "Experts" give a short talk about their unique topic, sharing something new and interesting. Encourage people to take notes. Then give the teams 10 minutes to develop at least three new products or services inspired by the new knowledge they have obtained.

Next, call on representatives from some of the groups to report on their results. Then lead a discussion about the importance of broad training for the creative process.

Discussion Questions

1. Was the Expert's topic unique or unusual in some way? How so?
2. Could you have developed the same products (or services) without the help of the Expert?
3. Why is broad training important for creativity?

Tip!

It may be a little tricky at first to find your experts, but remember, everyone is an expert on *something*. It may be stamps, World War II, or even Superman comics.

FEEDBACK AND RECOGNITION:
DESIGN CHALLENGE

In a Nutshell

Participants design and carry out their own exercise to demonstrate how *feedback and recognition* can stimulate creativity.

Time

Allow at least 40-60 minutes. If you want to have a discussion after the game is complete (see below), plan on about 90 minutes for the whole process.

What You'll Need

The materials will vary with the task that the group designs. Have basic writing materials, a flipchart, and some odd objects on hand–the basics you need for all design challenges.

What to Do

The participants' task is to design and implement at least one new game that shows how individuals can interact with others to encourage creative thinking or expression. Before you have them take on this challenge, be sure they have participated in at least one similar game, such as "The Tiny Little Nod Game," page 195.

Have people work in small teams, and give them at least 15 minutes in which to design the new game or games. Through a show of hands, see which teams had the most success with their designs, and then select one team to take charge of the whole group and try out one of their new games.

The game should demonstrate one or more of the following lessons: (a) feedback has an enormous impact on behavior, (b) even very subtle feedback can have an enormous impact on behavior, (c) showing approval for creative expression can accelerate creative expression, (d) showing disapproval for creative expression can stifle creative expression, (e) recognizing people for their creative efforts can increase those efforts, (f) recognizing the creative efforts of one person can increase the creative efforts of other people, or (g) failure to acknowledge or recognize creative expression can stifle creative expression.

After the game has been played, lead a brief discussion about what the game may have taught and how it could be improved. Also, find out about some of the other games that were designed.

If time allows, play another game or two that demonstrates the role that feedback and recognition play in creative expression.

Discussion Questions

1. How, in general, do feedback and recognition affect behavior?
2. How are feedback and recognition important for creativity?
3. How might a lack of feedback stifle creativity? How might negative feedback stifle creativity?
4. How easy was it to design your new game?
5. What method or methods did you use to get your design team to maximize its creative output?
6. How, if at all, did the game you played teach you about the role that feedback and recognition play in stimulating creativity?

And Don't Forget!

In a well-designed game, everyone should be able to participate or have fun, and time limits need to be respected. You may want to give the leadership team some tips to help make their game more successful. You might also announce that you're available to *participate* in the game they design.

FEEDBACK AND RECOGNITION:
WORKPLACE CHALLENGE

In a Nutshell

Participants work in teams to develop specific methods for improving *feedback* practices in their workplaces which will stimulate creativity.

Time

20-30 minutes.

What You'll Need

Writing materials, including blank sheets of paper (without lines), for each participant.

What to Do

Divide the group into small teams, and have the teams spend about 15 minutes compiling lists of methods that might improve feedback and recognition practices in their workplaces. If you like, use the "shifting" technique (see page 167) to enhance the creativity of your teams.

After the teams have finished, have representatives of different teams share their results with the group, and lead a discussion about how to improve feedback practices in the workplace. If your resources allow, collect the lists, compile them into a master list, and distribute it (by email, perhaps) to all participants.

Discussion Questions

1. To what extent are feedback and recognition currently used in your workplace to stimulate creativity?
2. How do feedback and recognition practices in your workplace currently help or hurt the creative process?
3. How might feedback and recognition practices in your workplace be improved to increase creativity?
4. What kind of training might your organization provide to teach people how to provide feedback and recognition in order to boost creativity?
5. What other methods might your organization use to teach people how to provide feedback and recognition for this purpose?
6. Which of your proposals are most feasible? Which are least feasible? How might you use creative problem-solving techniques to make the latter proposals more feasible?

And Don't Forget!

Some of your participants might feel that this is an exercise in futility—that limited resources or shortsighted managers will make it impossible to implement their suggestions. To those individuals you might point out: (1) that stating the suggestion is already a great step forward, (2) that resources and managers change from time to time, (3) that some suggestions can be implemented at little or no cost, and (4) that implementation problems are just more problems to be solved.

THE KEYS TO CREATIVITY (BASIC VERSION)

In a Nutshell

A volunteer tries to retrieve distant keys using a broom or mop.

Time

30-45 minutes.

What You'll Learn

(1) *Waiting* is important when you're looking for new ideas. Generative processes take time. (2) *Frustration* is a bothersome but essential part of the creative process. (3) *Failure* can accelerate the creative process. (4) *Reassurance* and *support* can help people persevere and succeed when faced with a difficult problem.

What You'll Need

A footstool, a key ring (1-inch inner diameter) with about five keys on it, masking tape, and a standard mop or broom. The broom (or mop) that you've chosen should have a standard wood handle which can be unscrewed from the head; most brooms are built this way. If your key ring, with the keys on it, is the correct size, it should be impossible for you to insert the handle end of the broom stick through the ring. Unscrewing the handle, you should find it easy to insert the screw end of the handle into the ring (since the screw end tapers toward a narrow end). You'll need a clear area in front of the room–roughly 10 feet wide and five feet deep–for your volunteer to work on the problem.

What to Do

Be sure the equipment for the game is out of sight. Then select a volunteer and send him or her out of the room.

Now, pull out the ring of keys and the *intact* broom (or mop). Inform the participants that the volunteers will have to retrieve the keys using the broom.

Next, set up the materials while telling the group what to expect. Place the footstool in front of the room, and put the ring of keys on the stool so that, from the vantage point of the volunteer, the ring protrudes upward like the letter O. Next, place a 4-foot length of masking tape on the floor about 6 feet away from the stool. Finally, place the mop or broom next to the masking-tape line, on the side opposite the stool (see diagram).

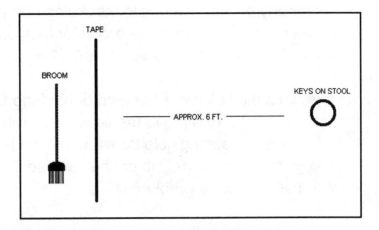

Inform the group that the volunteer's task will be to retrieve the ring of keys without crossing the line and without letting the keys touch the ground. Demonstrate the likely outcome: The volunteer will probably first try to spear the key ring with the handle end of the broom, but that won't work. Failure will produce various "extinction effects": frustration, variability in responding, and the reappearance of old forms of behavior ("resurgence").

At some point the volunteer might try to use the broom to pull or push the stool close to the line. Tell the group that you'll disallow this solution, telling the volunteer that it's "too costly."

Finally, unscrew the broom head and demonstrate the solution you're looking for: spearing the key ring with the tapered end of the broom handle. This might seem difficult, but so is the real world. What's more, people virtually always get this solution—given enough time.

Replace the broom or mop head, set up the keys again

properly (so that the ring looks like an upright O when you're behind the line), place the broom or mop on the floor beside the line, and call in the volunteer.

Instruct the volunteer to stand behind the line, and give the assignment: to retrieve the set of keys without crossing the line, without getting help from anyone, and without letting the keys touch the floor. He or she can use the broom (or mop) to help solve the problem.

If the keys fall to the floor, you'll need to position them again. Once the easy solution has been achieved (pulling the entire stool toward the line), congratulate the volunteer, restore the stool and keys to their original positions, and continue as follows: "Great job, but a memo has just come down from a Senior VP complaining about the costs involved in moving mountains. So you'll need to solve the problem another way, this time without moving the stool. Please continue."

The solution should emerge in the next 5 to10 minutes. Along the way, you may need to reassure the volunteer that the problem can actually be solved. The statement "You can do it!" may be all you'll need. Be patient and upbeat. Generative processes take time, and frustration is a sign that the processes are working.

When the solution has been reached, lead a discussion about what the volunteer did, said, and felt when faced with this problem.

Discussion Questions

1. How predictable was the volunteer's performance? In what ways was it surprising?
2. How does this exercise demonstrate the importance of waiting?
3. Did you see signs of frustration at any point? Was frustration followed by constructive behavior at various times?
4. Did reassurances from the leader help the volunteer to persevere?
5. How did failure spur the volunteer's creativity?

If You Have More Time

Send two or three people out of the room and have them solve the problem one at a time.

Tips!

This exercise is every bit as fun as it is frustrating. Usually group members cheer on and support the volunteer through his or her ordeal. If time is tight, you might have to give the volunteer some subtle hints to help him or her solve the problem, but you're better off extending the exercise if you can.

People *always* solve the problem, given enough time. Sometimes the volunteer is lucky enough to snag the keys with the bristle end of the broom. If that happens, simply set things up again, congratulate the volunteer, and ask for yet *another* solution! (You can avoid the bristle problem by using a soft mop instead of the broom.)

THE KEYS TO CREATIVITY (ADVANCED VERSION)

In a Nutshell

A volunteer tries to retrieve a set of keys that are out of reach. The volunteer is provided with some materials that are helpful for solving the problem and with other materials that are irrelevant.

Time

30-45 minutes.

What You'll Learn

Multiple controlling stimuli lead to new ideas, but they can also delay the appearance of solutions to particular problems. In the real world, it's hard to tell the good stimuli from the bad.

What You'll Need

A footstool, a key ring (1-inch inner diameter) with about 5 keys on it, masking tape, a standard mop or broom, and an assortment of children's toys. See the previous exercise for further details about the key ring and mop or broom.

What to Do

Follow the instructions in the Basic Version of this exercise (previous chapter), with this exception: Before bringing in the volunteer, place a number of children's toys or other interesting objects near the broom or mop—objects such as a plastic baseball bat, a set of dominoes, a tennis ball, a plastic ring, and so on. Ideally, these items should not be very useful for solving the problem. The more objects, the better.

Bring the volunteer into the room, and instruct him or her as follows: "Your task is to retrieve those keys. They mustn't touch the ground, and you cannot cross or walk around this line. You also cannot ask others to help you. You can use any of these objects"—now point to the assortment of objects—"to help you solve the problem."

If the volunteer stumbles onto a solution you hadn't anticipated, offer your congratulations, "requisition" the offending toy, and have the volunteer start again.

Discussion Questions

1. How did the irrelevant objects affect the volunteer? Did these objects delay the solutions to the problem? Did they lead to an interesting or novel behavior?
2. How were the conditions in this exercise like those of the real world? How were they unlike those of the real world?
3. This exercise shows that "multiple controlling stimuli"

spur creativity, but that they also delay the appearance of a solution. How does it show these things?

Alternative

If you want to explore the effects of using other distractors, repeat the exercise with a second volunteer.

Tips!

Be certain that the footstool is far enough behind the line so that people can't lean over to reach the keys and that it's close enough to allow people to reach the keys with the end of the mop or broom handle.

If you have lots of time, consider doing the basic and advanced versions of this exercise in sequence. Send two volunteers out of the room. Bring in the first one and do the basic version of the game. Then bring in the second volunteer and do the advanced version. You can also do either version on its own. Keep in mind that they teach different things, so pick the game that best suits your needs.

THE LOLA COLA GAME

In a Nutshell

Working in teams, participants invent names for a new cola. Some teams are given "open-ended" instructions, while other teams are given conventional, bounded instructions.

Time

20-25 minutes.

What You'll Learn

Open-ended instructions typically produce both *more* ideas and *more creative* ideas.

What You'll Need

Writing materials should be provided for all participants. Also, you'll need written instructions for all of your teams: one set for the Drunken Designers and another set for the Carbonated Creators. You can copy and cut the instructions on page 112 for this purpose.

What to Do

Divide the group into two subgroups, the Drunken Designers and the Carbonated Creators, and divide each subgroup up into teams of between three and five people.

Describe the task as follows: Lola, headstrong head of Research and Development, has developed a new cola, which, of course, she'd like to call "Lola Cola." You need to convince her that she's on the wrong track.

Distribute the written instructions to the Drunken Designers and the Carbonated Creators, and have them follow those instructions to prepare for their meeting with Lola.

If you like, you can have both types of teams use the "shifting" technique to maximize their creative output (see page 167).

Give the teams 15 minutes to carry out their instructions. Then call on representatives from some or all of the teams to present their reports. Keep track of two key numbers as each team presents its report: (1) the total number of new cola names developed in each group, and (2) the number of "fantastic" cola names developed in each group.

Explain to everyone how the instructions differed in the two subgroups, summarize the numbers you have collected. The chances are good that the Carbonated Creators–the teams receiving open-ended instructions–will have produced (1) more cola names (on the average) and (2) more "fantastic" cola names than were produced by the Drunken Designers–the teams receiving traditional bounded instructions. Lead a discussion about why open-ended instructions–instructions that explicitly say that solutions should be unlimited in one or more ways–produce more and better outcomes than do traditional bounded instructions–instructions that either state or imply boundaries on creativity.

Discussion Questions

1. Did the Drunken Designers perform differently than the Carbonated Creators? How so?
2. What are open-ended instructions? How are they different from traditional instructions?
3. What types of instructions, goals, and tasks, are you usually given in your work setting–open-ended or bounded? Give some examples.
4. Why do open-ended instructions typically produce more and better ideas than do bounded instructions?
5. How might instructions in your work setting be improved to produce more and better ideas?

Alternative

If you like, you can appoint a panel of judges to judge the "creativeness" of the cola names produced by the two subgroups. The Carbonated Creators–the teams receiving open-ended instructions–will probably produce names judged, on the average, to be more creative than those produced by the Drunken Designers.

You can also use the Lola Cola framework to conduct a game that shows the power of the "shifting" technique (compare "The Shifting Game," page 167).

Tip!

"Bridges to Creativity" (page 45) uses a different task to demonstrate the power of open-ended instructions. Since each relies on written instructions, you can, if you like, use both games with the same group.

Instructions for the Drunken Designers

Lola, Director of R&D, wants to name her new cola "Lola Cola." Fifteen minutes from now, a representative from your team must present Lola with a succinct report that will convince her to proceed with a better name. In the next 15 minutes, your team needs to invent roughly five new cola names and then to present the following brief report to Lola:

> *Hi, Lola. We're pleased to report that our team, the Drunken Designers, has developed _____ [mention number here] possible new names for the company's new cola, _____ [mention number here] of which we think are truly fantastic. Our fantastic new cola names are _____ [give the names]. Thanks for your consideration!*

-------- ✂ --------

Instructions for the Carbonated Creators

Lola, Director of R&D, wants to name her new cola "Lola Cola." Fifteen minutes from now, a representative from your team must present Lola with a succinct report that will convince her to proceed with a better name. In the next 15 minutes, your team needs to invent as many new cola names as possible and then to present the following brief report to Lola:

> *Hi, Lola. We're pleased to report that our team, the Carbonated Creators, has developed _____ [mention number here] possible new names for the company's new cola, _____ [mention number here] of which we think are truly fantastic. Our fantastic new cola names are _____ _____ [give the names]. Thanks for your consideration!*

112

MANAGING RESOURCES:
DESIGN CHALLENGE

In a Nutshell

Participants design and carry out their own exercise to demonstrate that *resource management* is important for creative expression.

Time

Allow at least 40-60 minutes. If you want to have a discussion after the game is complete (see below), plan on about 90 minutes for the whole process.

What You'll Need

The materials will vary with the task that the group designs. Have basic writing materials, a flipchart, and some odd objects on hand.

What to Do

The participants' task is to design and implement at least one new game that shows how important resource management is for the creative process. Before you have them take on this challenge, be sure they have participated in at least one similar game, such as "The Popsicology Game," page 153.

Have people work in small teams, and give them at least 15 minutes in which to design the new game or games. Through a show of hands, see which teams had the most success with their designs, and then select one team to take charge of the whole group and try out one of their new games.

The game should demonstrate one or more of the following lessons: (a) that a lack of material or human resources can stifle creativity, (b) that ample material and human resources can accelerate creativity, or (c) that the *type* of new ideas people have is determined in part by the *nature* of the resources to which they have access.

After the game has been played, lead a brief discussion about what the game may have taught and how it could be improved. Also, find out about some of the other games that were designed.

If time allows, play another game or two that demonstrates the importance of resource management for creativity.

Discussion Questions

1. How are material and human resources important for creativity?
2. How might a lack of material or human resources stifle creativity?
3. How might ample material and human resources accelerate creativity?
4. How might the type of new ideas that people have be determined by the nature of the resources to which they have access?
5. How easy was it to design a new game?

6.   What method or methods did you use to get your design team to maximize its creative output?
7.   How, if at all, did the game you played teach you about managing resources to stimulate creativity?

And Don't Forget!

In a well-designed game, everyone should be able to participate or at least have some fun, and time limits need to be respected. You may want to give the leadership team some tips to help make their game more successful. On the other hand, for extra fun for both you and the group, you might also announce that you're available to *participate* in the team-designed game.

MANAGING RESOURCES:
WORKPLACE CHALLENGE

In a Nutshell

Participants work in teams to develop specific methods for optimizing creativity in their workplaces through better management of human and material resources.

Time

20-30 minutes.

What You'll Need

Writing materials, including blank sheets of paper (without lines), for each participant.

What to Do

Divide the group into small teams, and have the teams spend about 15 minutes compiling lists of methods that might enhance the management of human and material resources in their workplaces for the purpose of stimulating creativity. If you like, use the "shifting" technique (see page 167) to enhance the creativity of your teams.

After the teams have finished, have representatives of different teams share their results with the group, and lead a discussion about how to improve capturing in the workplace. If your resources allow, collect the lists, compile them into a master list, and distribute it (by email, perhaps) to all participants.

Discussion Questions

1. To what extent are human and material resources in your workplace currently managed so as to stimulate creativity?
2. How does the management of resources in your workplace currently help or hurt the creative process?
3. How might resource management in your workplace be improved to increase creativity?
4. What kind of training might your organization provide to teach people how to provide feedback or recognition so as to manage resources better in order to boost creativity?
5. What other methods might your organization use to teach people how to manage resources better for this purpose?
6. Which of your proposals are most feasible? Which are least feasible? How might you use creative problem-solving techniques to make the latter proposals more feasible?

And Don't Forget!

Some of your participants might feel that this is an exercise in futility–that limited resources or shortsighted managers will make it impossible to implement their suggestions. To those individuals you might point out that: (1) stating the suggestion is already a great step forward, (2) resources and managers change from time to time, (3) some suggestions can be implemented at little or no cost, and (4) implementation problems are just more problems to be solved.

MANAGING TEAMS:
DESIGN CHALLENGE

In a Nutshell

Participants design and carry out their own exercise to demonstrate that *team management* practices make a difference in the creative output of a team.

Time

Allow at least 40-60 minutes. If you want to have a discussion after the game is complete (see below), plan on about 90 minutes for the whole process.

What You'll Need

The materials will vary with the task that the group designs. Have basic writing materials, a flipchart, and some odd objects on hand.

What to Do

The participants' task is to design and implement at least one new game that shows that the creative output of a team depends on how that team is managed. Before you have them take on this challenge, be sure they have participated in at least one similar game, such as "The Shifting Game," page 167.

Have people work in small teams, and give them at least 15 minutes in which to design the new game or games. Through a show of hands, see which teams had the most success with their designs, and then select one team to take charge of the whole group and try out one of their new games.

The game should demonstrate one or more of the following lessons: (a) Teams can both inhibit and accelerate creativity. (b) Creativity is fundamentally an individual phenomenon, not a group phenomenon. (c) The members of a team can help stimulate new ideas in an individual by providing unusual or multiple stimuli for that individual (see material on "surrounding," page 17 [introductory chapter], or see "The Shifting Game," page 167). (d) Team members can inhibit creativity by showing disapproval when someone expresses a new idea. (e) "Role playing" can be helpful in getting people to express new ideas in a group setting. (f) Shifting in and out of a group greatly increases the overall creative output of that group (see "The Shifting Game," page 167). (g) Groups are better at selecting good ideas than they are at generating them (see "The Team as Quality Editor," page 187).

After the game has been played, lead a brief discussion about what the game may have taught and how it could be improved. Also, find out about some of the other games that were designed.

If time allows, play another game or two that demonstrates that proper team management is important for the creative process.

Discussion Questions

1. How easy was it to design your new game?
2. What method or methods did you use to get your design team to maximize its creative output?
3. How, if at all, did the game you played teach you about managing teams?
4. How might your game be improved?

And Don't Forget!

In a well-designed game, everyone should be able to participate or at least have some fun, and time limits need to be respected. You may want to give the leadership team some tips to help make their game more successful. On the other hand, for extra fun for both you and the group, you might also announce that you're available to *participate* in the team-designed game.

MANAGING TEAMS:
WORKPLACE CHALLENGE

In a Nutshell

Participants work in teams to develop specific methods for optimizing creativity in their workplaces through better management of teams and workgroups.

Time

20-30 minutes.

What You'll Need

Writing materials, including blank sheets of paper (without lines), for each participant.

What to Do

Divide the group into small teams, and have the teams spend about 15 minutes compiling lists of methods that might improve the way teams are used in their workplaces to produce new ideas. If you like, use the "shifting" technique (see page 167) to enhance the creativity of your teams.

After the teams are done, have representatives of different

teams share their results with the group, and lead a discussion about how to improve team management in the workplace. If your resources allow, collect the lists, compile them into a master list, and distribute it (by email, perhaps) to all participants.

Discussion Questions

1. To what extent are teams in your workplace currently successful at generating new ideas?
2. How do current team management techniques in your workplace help or hurt the creative process?
3. How might team management techniques in your workplace be improved to increase the creative output of your teams?
4. What kind of training might your organization provide to teach people how to manage teams better in order to boost team creativity?
5. What other methods might your organization use to teach people how to manage teams better for this purpose?
6. Which of your proposals are most feasible? Which are least feasible? How might you use creative problem-solving techniques to make the latter proposals more feasible?

And Don't Forget!

Some of your participants might feel that this is an exercise in futility–that limited resources or shortsighted managers will make it impossible to implement their suggestions. To those individuals you might point out that: (1) stating the suggestion is already a great step forward, (2) resources and managers change from time to time, (3) some suggestions can be implemented at little or no cost, and (4) implementation problems are just more problems to be solved.

THE MEMORY GAME

In a Nutshell

Some people try to remember their new ideas, while others write them down on Memory Pads.

Time

About 15 minutes.

What You'll Learn

Supplying people with "capturing tools"–tools for recording their new ideas as they occur–can vastly increase creative output.

What You'll Need

Writing materials for half the participants–preferably including paper or a pad that's marked "Memory Pad" or "New Ideas" at the top. A blackboard or flipchart would also be helpful, along with a timer or stopwatch.

What to Do

This is a deceptively simple, yet informative, exercise. Working individually or in small teams, everyone is given 10 minutes in which to name a new chewing gum. But half the group is allowed to record their ideas on paper, while the other half must try to remember their new ideas.

When the time is up, have a few people from each group come to the front of the room and write their lists on the blackboard. Typically, those who've been allowed to write their ideas will present at least three times as many ideas as those who tried to remember their ideas.

Lead a brief discussion about (a) the importance of preserving new ideas as they occur, (b) materials and supplies that could be used to promote capturing in the workplace or at home (paper, tape recorders, computers, pocket computers, cell phones, folders, notebooks, blackboards, erasable walls, special pens, etc.), and (c) management practices that might increase capturing in the workplace.

Discussion Questions

1. Who presented more ideas, those who recorded their ideas or those who tried to remember their ideas?
2. How big a difference was there in the creative output of these two groups?
3. Why is it important to have the right materials and supplies at hand when you're generating new ideas?

4. Do you currently have resources at hand which allow you to preserve new ideas when they occur to you? How might the capturing tools in your work environment be improved?

5. How might management practices in your work environment be improved so as to encourage employees to capture new ideas?

Tip!

The longer you have people work on the problem, the larger the difference you'll see in the two groups.

THE MONKEY-DO GAME

In a Nutshell

The group leader records some new ideas on the blackboard and fails to record other new ideas. Will the group imitate?

Time

About 15 minutes.

What You'll Learn

People often imitate the habits of an authority figure. If a leader uses good creativity management skills, others will tend to follow.

What You'll Need

Just a blackboard or flipchart. Participants will also need writing materials.

What Not to Do

Don't tell people that this activity is called "The Monkey-Do Game"! You can reveal this at the end, if you like. As a temporary cover, call the game "The Green-and-Yellow Game." In other words, lie.

What to Do

Before you start, make sure everyone has writing materials, and inform people that they might want to take some notes.

Now ask the group to help you name a new soft drink. Your company can produce the drink with either green coloring or yellow coloring, so you need two sets of names.

Ask people to raise their hands with their suggestions. Whenever you get a suggestion for a *green* drink, either *fail* to record that name on the blackboard or record it poorly–for example, in abbreviated form. Whenever you get a suggestion for a *yellow* drink, record that name accurately. Try to solicit an equal number of suggestions for each drink.

After a few minutes, erase the board completely (or, if you're using a flipchart, simply turn the page). Now ask people to raise their hands if they took notes on the discussion. Assuming that some people did, ask them to help you reconstruct the two lists based only on what they wrote down–in other words, not from memory.

Based on what people recorded, you should be able to construct an excellent list of possible new names for the yellow drink, but the green list will probably be fairly short and dull.

Finally, reveal the true purpose of the game: to show that people imitate the creativity management skills of other people—especially of people in positions of authority. Lead a brief discussion about how important it is for managers to know how to manage their own creativity.

Discussion Questions

1. Did the green and yellow lists turn out to be different? Why or why not?
2. Did people tend to copy what the leader was writing? How might this be a problem in a real work situation?
3. Why is it important for managers, supervisors, and other leaders to have good creativity competencies? How might the creativity of other people be limited if the manager's creativity competencies are weak?

Alternative

Without others knowing, appoint someone in the group to be your secret assistant, and have that individual keep a an accurate record of the green soft drink names. After you've had the group help you reconstruct the two lists, have your accomplice reveal the complete list of green names.

THE NEWS-YOU-CAN-USE GAME

In a Nutshell

Volunteers are given some information about newspapers and then asked to solve a simple problem using a newspaper.

Time

20-25 minutes.

What You'll Learn

Previous learning has an impact on the creative process. The more training people have had and the more diverse that training, the more creative they will be.

What You'll Need

Newspapers! One full-size daily is probably sufficient. You'll also need a small round balloon, a roll of tape, and copies of pages 139 and 140. A long table in the front of the room would be helpful but isn't essential.

What to Do

Select two volunteers and have them leave the room. Then inflate a balloon and place it at one end of the long table, so that it's too far away for someone to reach when he or she is standing at the other end of the table. If you prefer, you can place a line on the floor with a piece of masking tape and then place the balloon on the floor about six feet away from the line. Almost any arrangement will do, as long as the balloon is out of reach by two or three feet. Place the newspaper and roll of tape at the near end of the table (far from the balloon) or wherever it is that the volunteer is going to stand.

For dramatic effect, you may want to grab a marker at this point and label the balloon "BONUS" or "PROMOTION" or "BALLOON PAYMENT" or something along those lines.

Appoint a timekeeper, and instruct him or her to time the performance of each volunteer from the time you say "Begin" until the performance is completed. Then bring in the first volunteer.

Give a copy of page 139 (Form 1) to the first volunteer, and read the text aloud.

Instruct the volunteer to stand on the particular spot and, using the newspaper and tape, to retrieve the balloon as quickly as possible within the next 5 minutes. The volunteer may not use any other objects; he or she may not move out of this position; and he or she may not ask others for help.

When the participant has finished the task (or the maximum time has been reached), repeat this procedure with the second volunteer, this time using the handout on page 140 (Form 2).

The two handouts differ in only one significant respect: Form 2 includes instructions for rolling up a newspaper to make a fishing rod. The first volunteer may or may not know how to construct such a device; the second volunteer definitely has this information and thus should have an easier time solving the problem.

The solution to the problem is as follows: Roll up the newspaper tightly into a long rod (perhaps using the tape to secure it). Attach a piece of tape to the end of the rod so that a sticky surface is exposed. Extend the rod toward the balloon, touch the sticky surface to it, and retrieve the balloon.

Now, hold a discussion that focuses on the differences between the two performances. If the differences were minimal, or if the result was opposite from the expected one, your discussion should focus on explaining the outcome.

Discussion Questions

1. What was the difference in the two types of "training" the volunteers received?
2. Did different training produce different outcomes? Why or why not?
3. Why does previous learning affect creativity?

4.   How can you direct creativity toward useful ends by providing certain training?

Alternative

You can conduct this entire game as a *gedunken* game (or "thought" game), without any props. Paper and pencil will do. The two types of instructions can be distributed on paper, one to each half of the group, and everyone can participate.

If you're using a balloon, you can add spice (and noise) to the proceedings by changing the goal: Instead of instructing the volunteers to retrieve the balloon, tell them that their mission is to pop it.

THE NEWS-YOU-CAN-USE GAME
Form 1

Here are five possible uses for a newspaper. Please study them carefully.

1) You can read it and learn about news, entertainment, and bargains.

2) You can cover your head with it during a sudden rainstorm.

3) You can line your bird cage with it.

4) You can tear it into strips and use it to start your camp fire.

5) You can wad it and use it as packing material.

THE NEWS-YOU-CAN-USE GAME
Form 2

Here are five possible uses for a newspaper. Please study them carefully.

1) You can read it and learn about news, entertainment, and bargains.

2) You can cover your head with it during a sudden rainstorm.

3) You can line your bird cage with it.

4) You can roll a page of it up tightly to make a fishing pole.

5) You can tear it into strips and use it to start your camp fire.

140

THE NO-HANDS GAME

In a Nutshell

Participants use *feedback* to try to get
a volunteer to move his or her *hands*,
while the leader uses *instructions* to
try to get the volunteer to move his or her *legs*.

Time

15 minutes.

What You'll Learn

Feedback is often much more powerful than rules or
instructions–even instructions from an authority figure.

What You'll Need

Just a sense of humor.

What to Do

Pick a volunteer, then ask him or her to leave the room. Have
the group pick a Target Behavior that uses *hands*, such as

clapping overhead or doing chicken flaps. Bring the volunteer back, and explain that the group is going to try to get him or her do something that involves his *legs*. The group will shout "Yes!" whenever he or she does something close to the desired target. (This is called a "shaping" task, in which closer and closer approximations to a target behavior are reinforced, in this case with the word "Yes!")

Because of the leader's instructions, the volunteer will keep moving his or her legs, but the group will shout "Yes!" only when he or she moves his or her *hands*. The feedback from the group will usually overwhelm the leader's instructions. The leader can interrupt at various points, insisting in increasingly stronger language that the group really wants the volunteer to move his or her *legs* and that he or she *mustn't* move his or her hands.

This game produces lots of tension and laughter, as the leader's instructions compete with the audience's feedback – with the feedback usually winning.

Discussion Questions

1. What happens when feedback competes with instructions? Which one usually wins?
2. What are examples from everyday life in which feedback is in competition with instructions? How does the Surgeon General's warning on cigarette packs compete with the actual consequences of smoking a cigarette?
3. What was the outcome of the exercise? What did it

show about the power of feedback?

4. Why is it not enough for supervisors to ask people to express creativity?   What else must they do to encourage creativity? How can feedback be used for this purpose?

THE NOT-FOR-THE-FAINTHEARTED GAME

In a Nutshell

The entire group uses a "shaping" procedure to teach a volunteer to do something and then allows the volunteer to fail for a few minutes.

Time

20 minutes.

What You'll Learn

Failure ("extinction") plays an important role in the emergence of novel behavior.

What You'll Need

No special materials or supplies are needed.

What to Do

Part One: *Embarrass the Group Leader.*

Inform the participants that you're going to leave the room briefly. Tell them that while you're out of the room, they'll need to pick something simple but unusual for you to do when you return (like turning in circles or taking off your shoes). Then tell them that once you enter the room, they can't *tell you or show you* what you're supposed to do. All they can do is shout "Yes!"–preferably, in unison.

Explain that, at first, they should shout "Yes!" whenever they see you doing anything even remotely like the target behavior. For example, if they're trying to get you to touch your nose, they should shout "Yes!" when you move your hand even slightly upward. Then they should shout "Yes" when, over time, they see closer and closer approximations to the target behavior–for example, hand movements closer and closer to the nose. Remind the group that there's *no* saying *"No."* Have everyone practice the shout a few times to get them warmed up.

Now pick a volunteer to help the group select the target behavior, and tell the volunteer that he or she should bring you back into the room after the group has made its selection. Leave the room. After a few minutes, the volunteer will retrieve you, and you should have some fun while the group "shapes" your behavior with shouts of "Yes!"

Part One of the game demonstrates how positive reinforcement, used in a shaping procedure, can get someone to behave in new ways. More generally, it also shows the power of reinforcement for changing behavior. Although these are important lessons, Part Two of the game teaches an even more important one.

Part Two: *Embarrass the Volunteer.*

Select a volunteer—preferably someone outgoing and energetic—and send him or her out of the room. Then solicit suggestions for a new target behavior. Don't pick a behavior that's too easy or obvious. You're better off with something strange–for example, having someone pick up a chair, carry it across the room, and put it on a table.

Now explain to everyone that this exercise is just like "Embarrass the Group Leader," with one twist. After you bring the volunteer into the room, you'll stand *with your hands down* while the group shapes the target behavior. After a few minutes–when the target behavior has been achieved or nearly achieved–you'll *cross your arms*. This is the signal for the group to *stop saying yes*.

For the next few minutes, everyone should just observe the volunteer as he or she tries to figure out what to do. This is a period in which the volunteer is "failing"–in which his or her behavior is "undergoing extinction." See if members of the group can predict what the volunteer will do during this period.

Having explained this, bring the volunteer into the room, and proceed as outlined above.

Following an extinction period of a few minutes, lead a discussion about what you observed. Did the volunteer repeat old behaviors that had been reinforced? Were there signs of frustration? Did new behaviors emerge?

When you're done, be sure to offer the volunteer a hearty thanks and congratulations. Failure is frustrating, even for a few minutes!

Discussion Questions

1. Did you see any signs of frustration?
2. After the reinforcers stopped, did the volunteer repeat any behaviors that had been reinforced during the period of shaping? What did he or she do? (This phenomenon is called "resurgence." See Chapter 1 of this book for details.)
3. Did the volunteer do any new things after the supply of reinforcers was cut off? What new behaviors appeared? How did they relate to behaviors that were reinforced during the shaping period?
4. Failure has both positive and negative effects in this game. Can you give some examples?

Tip!

Don't let the group select target behaviors that involves long sequences of actions. And don't let them pick vocal behavior for this particular game; stick with movement.

THE ODD COUPLE GAME

In a Nutshell

Dice are used to help people pair up different products and odd topics. Based on the pairing, people try to improve existing products or to invent new ones.

Time

45-60 minutes.

What You'll Learn

Pairing a current task with a topic that's very different from that task helps people think in new ways.

What You'll Need

Writing materials for all participants, as well as one copy of a Matching Sheet for every team. You can use the sheet on page 151 if you like, or you can make your own. You'll also need one pair of dice for every team. Ideally, the dice in each pair should be of different colors, with one color for "product" and the other for "topic." A timer would also be helpful.

What to Do

Divide the group up into small teams, and give each team a Matching Sheet and a pair of dice. Have them roll the dice to pair a product with a topic (a roll of 2-4, for example, would pair "Computer Monitors" with "Elvis"). Then, based on that pairing, give them 5 minutes in which to improve that product or to invent an entirely new one.

When the time is up, have the teams roll the dice again to create another product-topic pair to work on (this might take several rolls).

Continue this process until all of the pairs have been exhausted. Then have representatives from each team present some of the new product ideas, and lead a discussion about the importance of broad training for creativity.

Discussion Questions

1. How was your thinking affected when you paired a product (like hats) with an unlikely topic (like insects)?
2, Do you routinely think about odd topics when you're working on a problem or trying to think of something new? What value might this have?
3. If you increased your knowledge in areas well outside of your current areas of expertise, how might this help you be creative?

MATCHING SHEET

Instructions: Roll the pair of dice to tell you which product to pair with which topic. Then draw a line connecting that product with that topic. Continue rolling until you've identified five pairs. The sixth one is the pair that's left over.

<u>Product</u>   <u>Topic</u>

Hairspray - 1   1 - The Civil War

Computer Monitors - 2   2 - Insects

Hats - 3   3 - Earwax

Breathmints - 4   4- Elvis

Earrings - 5   5 - The North Pole

Potato Chips - 6   6 - Witches

THE POPSICOLOGY GAME

In a Nutshell

Participants are asked to generate a creative design using popsicle sticks.

Time

20 minutes.

What You'll Learn

The more resources people have to develop their ideas, the more numerous and diverse those ideas.

What You'll Need

30 popsicle sticks for each pair of teams.

What to Do

This is a deceptively simple game. First select a panel of between three and five people to serve as the Judicious Judges. Divide the remaining group in two, with the Perky Picassos on one side of the room and the Marvelous Monets on the other. Now divide each of these groups into teams of about five people each.

Give each of the Perky Picasso teams 10 popsicle sticks, and give each of the Marvelous Monet teams 20 popsicle sticks. Now give everyone 5 minutes to generate the most creative design possible using only their popsicle sticks.

Finally, have the Judicious Judges circulate among the groups, rate each design, and then report their results to the entire group.

Discussion Questions

1. Which group developed the most creative designs, the Perky Picassos or the Marvelous Monets? Why?
2. How could the results of this game be applied to your workplace?

Alternative

Instead of popsicle sticks, use materials you may already have: Toothpicks, tongue depressors, raw spaghetti, etc.

Tips!

This game normally produces dramatic results. Why? Imagine that the sticks can only be placed side by side, either in the vertical or horizontal position (in fact, there are many more possibilities than these). In this restricted task, the Perky Picassos (with only 10 sticks per team) can produce 1,024 (2^{10}) different arrangements, but the Marvelous Monets (with 20 sticks per team) can produce

1,048,576 (2^{20}) different arrangements– and that's a very conservative look at the difference in possible outcomes in the two groups.

THE RANDOM DOODLES GAME

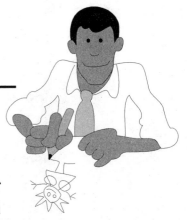

In a Nutshell

Participants generate random doodles and then try to remember them, with or without the benefit of a memorandum.

Time

15 minutes.

What You'll Learn

New ideas are fleeting. It's difficult to preserve them unless we record them immediately.

What You'll Need

A standard large pad (the flipchart type) mounted on an easel, some markers, and some strong tape (masking tape will do). In a small group, sheets of paper will suffice. Before you begin the game, draw lines on each sheet (six sheets for each volunteer) then divide each sheet into equal thirds, as shown in the diagram on page 159. A stopwatch will also be helpful.

What to Do

Remind participants that new ideas surge through our heads throughout the day. Some have value and some do not, but unless we capture those ideas, we'll never be able to assess their value.

Select two volunteers. Two easels should be set up in the front of the room, and both volunteers should draw at the same time. (The instructions below will assume that two people are drawing. With enough easels, you can have as many artists as you like. You can even do the exercise with just one lone volunteer.)

Ask the volunteers to draw some items, some of which will be real and some of which will be imaginary. When you announce the name of each item, have the volunteer write that name in the top and bottom thirds of the sheet of paper. Then have the volunteer draw that item in the *top third* section of the paper (see the diagram on page 159).

After a drawing is complete, fold the paper upwards as shown, and tape the sheet closed, so that only the bottom third of the paper is showing. Now give the volunteers another item to draw. Give six words in all—three real and three imaginary. If you like, select from the following lists:

Real	Imaginary	
TREE	ORK	JUB
HOUSE	ZIL	NID
CAR	GAK	EEF
DOG	YUG	KIF
GIRL	VEB	MIP
TABLE	ILM	ORZ

When all of the drawings have been completed and covered as shown, arrange for a delay in the proceedings–perhaps to take a bathroom break or to have a discussion about creativity in the news.

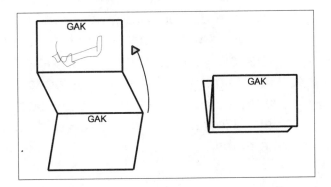

After a delay of five to ten minutes, recall the volunteers to the easels and ask them to draw the objects again, as you repeat the object names in a new order. The volunteers should make their new drawing in the bottom third of each piece of paper–the portion that remained showing after the paper was folded and taped.

Finally, when all the drawings are complete, remove the tape, and compare the old and new drawings.

For real objects, the old and new drawings will usually be similar. For imaginary objects, you will probably find little or no correspondence between the old and new drawings. New ideas are especially difficult to remember, which is why it's so important that we capture them as soon as they occur.

Discussion Questions

1. Why do you think novel ideas are so difficult to remember?
2. Can you think of a time when a great idea occurred to you and then disappeared, never to return? (It's interesting that we can often remember the incident but not the idea.)
3. What did you learn from this game?
4. How might you improve the odds that you'll be able to capture new ideas when they occur to you during the day? How might you preserve ideas that occur to you in the night?

Alternatives

This game can be done in many different ways. The way described above is actually fairly elaborate. You can make the same point by having everyone in the group draw a doodle, cover it, and then, some time later, try to draw it again. It's tough to do! (Try it and see!)

You need not even use drawings. You can have people make up their own nonsense syllables and try to remember them later, or you can have them generate random numbers and try to remember them. The point is that any novel behavior you ask people to generate will be very difficult for them to remember.

Tip!

Remember, novel ideas are like rabbits: They move swiftly,

and before you know it, they're gone. Not every new idea has value, of course, but if you want to produce more genuinely creative material, it helps to start with a larger pool of novel ideas. So preserve first, and evaluate later.

SELLING A ZORK

In a Nutshell

Participants are asked to sell a strange object to the group.

Time

15 minutes.

What You'll Learn

Unusual stimuli generate unusual ideas.

What You'll Need

The sky is the limit. The "Zork" can be almost anything, as long as it's unusual. You should have three objects (or drawings or photos) ready for each of the volunteer salespeople in the game. The items should be placed out of sight in front of the room before the game begins. If you're using a photo or drawing, you may want to use an overhead projector to display it to the group.

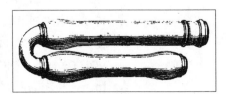

What to Do

Ask a volunteer come to the front of the room and face the audience. Explain that you will be showing him or her a "Zork" and that he or she will then have 3 minutes in which to sell the Zork to group for at least $250,000.

Show the Zork to the volunteer, and time the performance.

As time allows, repeat the procedure with other volunteers and other Zorks from your collection. With a suitable selection of objects, everyone should have great fun.

Discussion Questions

1. How is it that we're able to sell Zorks, even though we've never seen them before?
2. Is Zork-selling "creative"? Why or why not?
3. If you can sell a Zork, what else might you able to do that you're not doing now?
4. How, if at all, might Zork-selling be relevant to creativity in your personal or professional life?

Tip!

The more provocative and interesting the selection of Zorks, the more successful this game will be. Check your garage, the attic, or the Internet for the oddest stuff you can find. If all else fails, copy the Zorks we've included on the pages of this chapter!

THE SHIFTING GAME

In a Nutshell

Some participants work together as a team to generate names for a new product, while other participants shift in and out of a team while performing the same task.

Time

30-45 minutes.

What You'll Learn

Participants learn that (a) the creative process is an individual phenomenon, not a group phenomenon, (b) groups can stifle the creative process, and (c) shifting in and out of a group can maximize the creative output of that group.

What You'll Need

Two flipcharts would be helpful, as well as a clock or stopwatch. Participants will need writing materials. Mark one flipchart "Shifters" and the other "Togethers," and place each in front of the room.

What to Do

Divide the group into two subgroups, the Togethers and the Shifters, and divide each subgroup into teams of about five people each.

Announce the task that each team must tackle: "McDonald's is going to introduce the first fast-food non-fat hamburger. Think of as many names as you can for this new hamburger."

Now proceed with your instructions. Both the Togethers and the Shifters will have 20 minutes in which to complete the task. But the Togethers must stay together and work as a team during this time period, while the Shifters must shift in an out of their teams, as follows: At first, everyone works on the task individually (they can go to different parts of the room or even leave the room if they wish); then they come together into their teams for 5 minutes, then shift apart for five, then come together for five.

You might want to sound a bell to let the Shifters know that the time has come to shift, and you might also want to have some assistants on hand to help you herd Shifters in and out of their teams.

When the time is up, have representatives from each Shifters team copy their lists onto the Shifters flipchart, while representatives from each Togethers team copy their lists onto the Togethers flipchart. To save time, you can also get a quick count from each of the teams: How many hamburger names were generated in each group?

Note any differences in the output of the two subgroups, and ead a discussion about the advantages and disadvantages of shifting. Typically, the Shifters will produce between 50 and 100 percent more names than the Togethers, even though the Shifters have "wasted" much of their time moving around the room. Note that each type of group uses the same resources: The same number of people work on the problem over the same period of time.

Discussion Questions

1. Which subgroup produced more ideas, the Shifters or the Togethers? If you found a difference, why do you think it occurred?
2. Which subgroup produced "better" ideas? How might you test this?
3. In general, a shifting team produces both more ideas and better ideas than a non-shifting one. Why?
4. How does a team foster creativity among its members?
5. How does a team hinder creativity among its members?

If You Have More Time

Try multiple shifts—for example, six periods alternating between individual creativity and team creativity. Generally speaking, the more the shifts, the greater the differences between the Shifters and the Togethers.

Tip!

Remember, creativity is an individual phenomenon, not a group phenomenon. All new ideas spring from individual brains.

THE SRTCDJGJKLERED GAME

In a Nutshell

Participants tell a story using Word Ticklers–nonsensical strings of alphabet letters that are difficult to pronounce.

Time

5-15 minutes.

What You'll Learn

Unusual or ambiguous stimuli help get the creative juices flowing. And everyone–yes, *everyone*–has enormous creative potential.

What You'll Need

Slips of paper containing sentences that tell a simple story, slips of paper or cards containing Word Ticklers, and a handout for the group containing all of the Word Ticklers. In place of a handout, the Ticklers can be projected on a screen using an overhead projector. Pages 174 and 175 can be used to create these materials.

What to Do

Recruit five volunteers to be Storytellers, and give each of them (a) a slip of paper containing part of the story and (b) a slip of paper containing a Word Tickler. Next, distribute the list of Word Ticklers (but not the story!) to the entire group, or display the list of Word Ticklers (but not the story!) on a screen using an overhead projector or computer display.

Now, ask the Storytellers to tell the audience the story you've given them, entitled "How Pat Got Promoted from a Mail-Room Job to the Presidency of the Company." Going from left to right down the row of Storytellers, have each volunteer tell a piece of the story. Have them use the nonsense words you've provided to fill in the blanks.

Discussion Questions

1. Can people generate real language from random strings of alphabet letters? Why do you think this is possible?
2. The alphabet strings ("Word Ticklers") in this exercise are ambiguous. How do ambiguous stimuli help (or hurt) the creative process?
3. What other effects do ambiguous or unusual stimuli have? How do they make you feel?
4. Do you encounter ambiguous stimuli at work? What effect do they have on you?

If You Have More Time

To continue the game, have the storytellers trade slips and retell the story, or introduce another story of your own creation.

If You're Short on Time

You can use the Word Ticklers without any stories to support them. Simply ask participants to pronounce the Ticklers on page 175, perhaps by going around the table. Different people will pronounce the same Tickler in very different ways. For example, "tkeldifleowdnd" might become "Took a little fall. Oh, darned!" or "Take a daffodil down to Dad." Another variation: You can ask participants to create a complete sentence from each Tickler. In a business environment, you can ask participants to generate a new product or service from each Tickler.

Tip!

By the way, *just what is the name of this game?* The "Stick-a-Dagger-in-a-Juggler" Game? The "Sort-Your-CD's-from-Black-to-Red" Game? The "Stretch-Your-Jug-of-Liquor" Game? The "Steal-Your-Dog's-Licorice" Game? The "Scare-Away-the-Joker" Game? The "Race-Your-Dad-to-the-Fridge" Game? The "Try-to-Dance-a-Jig" Game? The "Try-to-Dig-for-Gold" Game? It's hard to say, really.

HOW PAT GOT PROMOTED FROM A MAIL-ROOM JOB
TO THE PRESIDENCY OF THE COMPANY

Pat had been a stamp-licker in the mail room for fourteen years. One day, when Pat went outside for a Twinkie break, a limousine carrying the President of the company ran over Pat's toes. This was a turning point in Pat's career. Pat exclaimed—well, shouted actually, "_____!"

- -

Pat's best friend, Sal, was a very, very close friend—if you know what I mean—of Jo, who was the President's trusted Senior Executive Assistant, and who also happened to be the one who actually did all of the President's work. Jo's toes had also been run over recently, so Jo was only too happy to work with Sal and Pat to replace the President. Jo didn't want the job, because Jo was too smart for that. So they made a plan, which Jo, always the joker, called "The _____ Plan."

- -

The Plan involved the usual stuff: a phony memo, a rumor about impending layoffs, some anonymous email messages about the President's dietary preferences, and a brilliant suggestion from Pat—deposited into the Suggestion Box in the mail room—that saved the company from financial ruin. The President, understandably upset by all this, could only comment, "_____." (After all, the President had used the same technique to become President just a few years before.)

- -

The same day Pat's name was placed on the President's office door, Pat thanked Sal and Jo in a most unusual way—yes, that's right, by _____. Wow, what a mess!

- -

Now Jo still runs the company, and Pat has fun running over the toes of people who work in the mail room. The moral of the story, of course, is _____.

WORD TICKLERS

-- ✂

1

okcceljalsfjeeijenc

-- ✂

2

ynnwhilzokoooehodwhsqd

-- ✂

3

voenslwugawneifhslree

-- ✂

4

wovnensownghisdyehslei

STICKY BUSINESS

In a Nutshell

Teams compete in a design contest, but some teams don't have enough glue.

Time

30-45 minutes.

What You'll Learn

Poor resources make people "creative" in the mundane sense of that word: They might use existing materials in new ways, for example. With ample resources, however, people are far more likely to be able to plan and implement ideas that are truly significant.

What You'll Need

Lots of popsicle sticks or small pieces of colored construction paper cut into odd shapes. You'll also need one small bottle of white glue for every team. You'll need to prepare the bottles in advance: Half of the bottles should be about half full. The other bottles should be nearly empty, containing only a few drops of glue. Ideally, the bottles should be opaque so that participants can't see how much glue the bottles contain. Mark the nearly empty bottles with an upper-case "P" (for "Paupers") on the bottom of each one. Mark the half-full bottles with an upper-case "K" (for "Kings") on the bottom of each one.

What to Do

Divide the group up into small teams and distribute an equal number of popsicle sticks (or pieces of construction paper) to each team–the more the better. Supply each team with one bottle of glue. Don't tell people about the two types of bottles, and don't identify the alphabet letters. Give everyone 15 minutes in which to assemble "at least one original, creative work of art" using the supplied materials. Tell them that they can use only the materials you've supplied and that they can't share resources with other teams. If any of the Paupers ask for more glue, tell them they'll have to make due with what they have.

When the time is up, reveal the significance of the alphabet letters on the bottom of the glue bottles. Then have representatives from each team present their creations to the group, and lead a discussion about the importance of resources for the creative process.

Discussion Questions

1. Who produced more creative products, the Paupers or the Kings? Typically, the Kings will outperform the Paupers, producing both more designs and more creative designs.
2. Why do the Kings usually outperform the Paupers in this task?
3. How is this task analogous to tasks you face in your workplace? How do limited resources restrict your creativity in the workplace?
4, What kinds of resources might improve your workplace creativity?

178

If You Have More Time

Appoint a panel of judges, and have them rate the "creativeness" of the teams' creations on a scale from 1 to 10, where 10 means "exceptionally creative." Then compare the mean rating for the Paupers to the mean rating for the Kings. The Kings should outperform the Paupers considerably.

SURROUNDING:
DESIGN CHALLENGE

In a Nutshell . .

Participants design and carry out their own exercise to demonstrate the role that *surrounding* plays in the creative process.

Time

Allow at least 40-60 minutes. If you want to have a discussion after the game is complete (see below), plan on about 90 minutes for the whole process.

What You'll Need

The materials will vary with the task that the group designs. Have basic writing materials, a flipchart, and some odd objects on hand. Because surrounding involves stimulation by multiple or unusual stimuli, try to have a wide variety of materials available: photos, graphics, toys, magazines, and so on. Surrounding can also involve *social* stimuli, so you might want to have some odd *people* on hand–or at least some costumes or makeup.

What to Do

The participants' task is to design and implement at least one new game that shows how important *surrounding skills* are for the creative process. Before you have them take on this challenge, be sure they have participated in at least one similar game, such as "Selling a Zork," page 163.

Have people work in small teams, and give them at least 15 minutes in which to design the new game or games. Through a show of hands, see which teams had the most success with their designs, and then select one team to take charge of the whole group and try out one of their new games.

The game should demonstrate one or more of the following lessons: (a) creativity is enhanced when we're exposed to interesting stimuli, (b) creativity is enhanced when we're exposed to interesting *combinations* of stimuli, (c) creativity is enhanced when we're exposed to interesting people, (d) creativity is enhanced when we're exposed to interesting *combinations* of people, (e) creativity is enhanced when we *change* the stimuli that surround us.

After the game has been played, lead a brief discussion about what the game may have taught and how it could be improved. Also, find out about some of the other games that were designed.

If time allows, play another game or two that demonstrates the power of surrounding.

Discussion Questions

1. How easy was it to design your new game?
2. What method or methods did you use to get your design team to maximize its creative output?
3. How, if at all, did the game you played teach about surrounding?
4. How might this game be improved to teach people about surrounding?

182

5.   How can diverse and interesting stimuli in your environment help boost your creativity?

And Don't Forget!

In a well-designed game, everyone should be able to participate or at least have some fun, and time limits need to be respected. You may want to give the leadership team some tips to help make their game more successful. On the other hand, for extra fun for both you and the group, you might also announce that you're available to *participate* in the team-designed game.

SURROUNDING:
WORKPLACE CHALLENGE

In a Nutshell

Participants work in teams to develop specific methods for improving *surrounding* practices in their workplaces.

Time

20-30 minutes.

What You'll Need

Writing materials, including blank sheets of paper (without lines), for each participant.

What to Do

Divide the group into small teams, and have the teams spend about 15 minutes compiling lists of methods that might enhance surrounding skills in their workplaces. If you like, use the "shifting" technique (see page 167) to enhance the creativity of your teams.

After the teams are done, have representatives of different teams share their results with the group, and lead a discussion about how to improve capturing in the workplace. If your resources allow, collect the lists, compile them into a master list, and distribute it (by email, perhaps) to all participants.

Discussion Questions

1. How can the surroundings in your organization be improved to stimulate creativity?
2. Does your plan include provisions for changing the surroundings periodically? Why is this important?
3. Does your present work environment help or hurt creativity? How so?
4. Which of your proposals are most feasible? Which are least feasible? How might you use creative problem-solving techniques to make the latter proposals more feasible?

And Don't Forget!

Some of your participants might feel that this is an exercise in futility–that limited resources or shortsighted managers will make it impossible to implement their suggestions. To those individuals you might point out that: (1) stating the suggestion is already a great step forward, (2) resources and managers change from time to time, (3) some suggestions can be implemented at little or no cost, and (4) implementation problems are just more problems to be solved.

THE TEAM AS
QUALITY EDITOR

In a Nutshell

Participants vote for different lists of
names, some lists generated by
individuals and one list generated by a team.

Time

15 minutes.

What You'll Learn

Teams are extremely good at selecting new ideas. (In fact
they're generally better at selecting new ideas than they are
at generating them.)

What You'll Need

A blackboard or flipchart, and writing materials for each
participant. You'll also need a place for a group of five
people to hold a brief private meeting.

What to Do

Ask the participants to help you compile of list of names for
a new rock'n'roll band. Record their suggestions on the
blackboard until you have between 20 and 25 names. Then
ask for five volunteers to serve on a Special Editors Team.
Have them copy down the list from the board, and send them

out of the room to pick the three names they think are best.

While the Special Editors Team is gone, have everyone, working individually, write down their own top three picks. Then call on three people at random, and have them write their top three picks on the blackboard. Call the Special Editors Team back into the room, and have them list their own top three picks on the blackboard. You should now have four lists on the board, as follows:

EDITORS   INDIVIDUALS
1.   1.   1.   1.
2.   2.   2.   2.
3.   3.   3.   3.

Finally, by a show of hands, have the entire group vote for their favorite list, and post the number of votes below each list. (Ideally, the Special Editors Team should not be allowed to vote.)

Which list won? Normally, a team-selected list of new ideas is superior to an individually selected list of new ideas, at least in one important respect: It's likely to be preferred by the population of people from which the team is drawn. In other words, the Editors' list should win by a landslide.

Discussion Questions

1. Teams can both help and hurt the creative process. In what ways?
2. Teams serve an essential role as editors of creative output. What can a team accomplish that an individual cannot?
3. Was the Editors' list preferred by the group? Why or why not?

4. Are teams used in your organization to produce new ideas? Are teams used optimally to select good ideas? If not, what improvements can you suggest?

Tip!

Remember, creativity is an individual process, in the sense that ideas always arise in individuals. After all, generative mechanisms exist in a single brain, and, as we all know too well, groups don't have a brain. But it's important that the raw creative output from individuals be subjected to the scrutiny of teams, and it is in that sense that teams play an essential role in the creativity of an organization.

THE TELL-ME-A-STORY GAME

In a Nutshell

Participants have 5 minutes to compose a story that's suggested by an interesting design, given by the group leader.

Time

10 minutes.

What You'll Learn

The power that unusual stimuli have for the creative process.

What You'll Need

Writing materials for all participants, a projector, and a transparency of the design on page 193.

What to Do

Begin simply by showing the participants the design on page 193 on a projector screen. Next, inform the participants that they have 5 minutes to compose the most interesting story they can, that's suggested by the design.

After the 5 minutes are up, call on a few people to share their stories.

Discussion Questions

1. What was your story about?
2. Were you surprised at the contents of your story?
3. What effect did the design have on your creativity?
4. How could you apply the concept of unusual stimuli in your workplace?

THE TINY LITTLE NOD GAME

In a Nutshell

People work in pairs, with one
person speaking and the other listening. The listener tries
to get the speaker to say a particular sentence, just by
nodding slightly from time to time.

Time

15 minutes.

What You'll Learn

This verbal shaping game shows the power of even subtle
feedback in encouraging creative speaking and thinking. It
also shows the power of positive reinforcement.

What You'll Need

Just a timer and some patience. A wristwatch will do–for the
timer, not the patience.

What to Do

Divide the group up into pairs. In each pair, one person is
the Speaker and the other is the Listener. Have each
Listener write down a Target Sentence–a non-obvious
sentence that he or she would like the Speaker to say, such

as "Ford makes a great car" or "I love pizza with mushrooms."

Then explain the task: Feedback—even subtle feedback—is so powerful that it can have an enormous impact on speech and thinking. The Speaker's task is to speak about anything and everyone for several minutes, watching for feedback from the Listener. The Listener's task is to "shape" the speech of the Speaker by reacting positively—with a *tiny little nod*—whenever the Speaker says something approaching the Target Sentence. No other feedback is allowed. Be sure to demonstrate the *tiny little nod* to the group.

Whenever the Listener feels that the Speaker has reached or come close to the Target Sentence (e.g., "My favorite car is a Ford"), the Listener should raise his or her hand to signal that his or her pair has completed the task. As each pair finishes, you can announce this to the group. Give the group 5 minutes to try to reach their Target Sentences. Add another minute or two if it looks some pairs are close to finishing.

Typically more than half of the pairs will reach the target within the allotted time—with most people amazed that subtle feedback can have such a large effect so very quickly.

Call on various pairs to divulge their Target Sentences and to report on how close the Speaker came to reaching the target.

Discussion Questions

1. When you heard the instructions for this game, did you think it would work? Could a tiny little nod possibly be enough to get someone to say an arbitrary sentence

in a few minutes time?

2. How many pairs reached the Target Sentence? How many came close?

3. How do people provide subtle feedback in everyday life? How might this feedback be affecting people's speech and thinking?

4. How might subtle feedback affect both the development of and the expression of creative ideas?

If You Have More Time

You might want to have the pairs switch Speaker/Listener roles.

THE TOYS-AS-TOOLS GAME

In a Nutshell

Participants are asked to invent new children's toys, given either no toys to examine or many toys to examine.

Time

20-30 minutes.

What You'll Learn

A rich assortment of stimuli helps spur the creative process.

What You'll Need

An assortment of small children's toys, as diverse as possible. Be sure you have at least a dozen; the more, the better. You'll also need a table in front of the room on which to display the toys. None of the toys should be on display when you start the exercise. You might want to keep them all in a box just behind the table. The display of toys should be obscured by a partition, so that only about half of the participants can see the toys. You'll also need a blackboard or flipchart on which to collect your results. Participants will need writing materials.

What to Do

Have people sit so that half of them can see the table and half of them can't. Then place the toys on the table, and ask people to invent as many new toys as they can in the next 15 minutes, listing their inventions on paper.

Half of the participants will be relying on their memories to help them design new toys. The rest of the participants will have the benefit of being able to see the assortment of toys you have provided.

After 15 minutes have passed, ask people how many new ideas they've been able to generate, and ask a few people to describe some of their ideas.

Compute the average number of new toy ideas generated by the people in each half of the room. Did people with the view do better? Discuss the results with the group.

Discussion Questions

1. Did the presence of toys help people to invent new ones? Why or why not?
2. How do diverse stimuli accelerate the creative process?
3. What should you put on your desk to promote creativity?

Alternative

The game can also be conducted with pictures or drawings of toys, instead of with real toys. In this case, you won't need the partition or table.

Tip!

Try to arrange the seats so that you have the same number of people in the toys and no-toys conditions.

THE ULTIMATE CHALLENGE GAME

In a Nutshell

Participants solve ultimate, open-ended problems that have no solutions.

Time

5-10 minutes.

What You'll Learn

Open-ended problems have a considerable effect in spurring creativity.

What You'll Need

Writing materials for all participants.

What to Do

Give the participants 3 minutes to solve a problem. They may not come up with the perfect answer in that time, but it's important that they write down at least one answer—even if it seems a little silly. After the 3 minutes are up, ask several of them to share their answers with the group.

Assign the first problem: "Propose a way to eliminate all air pollution in this country within the next 30 days. You have 3 minutes. Go."

When 3 minutes have passed, call on some members of the group to share their ideas.

Discussion Questions

1. When faced with difficult questions, do people simply shut down? What does happen? How do people react?
2. What kinds of replies do people give? Are the replies entirely useless?
3. How do ultimate questions spur creativity? What is the underlying mechanism?
4. What are the ultimate challenges in our industry?
5. Could ultimate challenges be used by our company on a regular basis to develop new ideas? How so?

If You Have More Time

As time permits, pose some additional "ultimate" questions, such as:

Tell us how to build a machine that will allow people to travel in time.

Propose a way to send someone to the moon for the price of a subway token.

Mt. Everest is blocking your view. Propose a scheme for knocking it down.

You need to raise a billion dollars by tomorrow at noon. Tell us how you're going to do it.

Alternative

Add some ultimate questions that are relevant to your business, or ask the group to propose some questions of this sort. If you work for the telephone company, ask, "What will the perfect telephone be like 100 years from now?" Again, give participants 3 minutes to answer, and then discuss some of the answers.

Tip!

The key to success in this game is in reminding participants to write down at least one answer to every question posed. People always have answers, but they are often reluctant to share them. Socialization has its advantages, but it also has costs—especially when creativity is on the line.

THE ULTIMATE DESIGN GAME

In a Nutshell

Participants shift in and out of small teams with the goal of developing at least 10 ways to increase creativity and innovation in their organization by a factor of 10 or more within the next 10 work days.

Time

30-40 minutes.

What You'll Learn

It can take thousands of new ideas to yield one of value. To get a great idea, it helps to have a large pool to choose from.

What You'll Need

Writing materials for each participant.

What to Do

Have the participants break up into teams of between four and six people, making sure that everyone has writing materials.

After the teams are organized, ask the participants to develop a minimum of 10 methods for increasing creativity and innovation in your organization by a factor of 10 or more. In other words, if you usually get about five new ideas a week, you must now get at least 50 new ideas a week. What's more, these methods must be fully implemented and fully effective within the next 10 workdays; that means you must achieve this goal in 10 days or less. In other words, 2 weeks from now your organization must be a hotbed of new and exciting ideas, and your new procedures must guarantee that this high level of creative output will continue year-round.

To complete this task, have the participants work as individuals for 5 minutes, and then shift them into teams. If you want them to shift out and in again, that's up to you. Give them a total of 20 minutes to complete this task, then ask representatives of various teams to present their plans to the group.

Discussion Questions

1. Asking for a minimum number of ideas still suggests a limit on how many ideas people should produce. What limit is suggested, and why will many people infer that limit?
2. Were any good ideas generated in this exercise? What proportion of the ideas that were generated could actually be implemented?
3. Was shifting helpful? Why or why not?

Tip!

Whenever time is limited, the number of ideas will also be limited, and some people work more slowly than others. So don't be alarmed if there seems to be a shortage of ideas.

You may want to experiment with other forms of the instructions that might produce greater output, such as: "Give me between 10 and 20 ideas" or "Give me as many ideas as you possibly can."

THE WAITING GAME

The Whole Game In a Nutshell

This game is so simple that the whole thing fits in a nutshell. The game works best when it's used right before a break or at the very end of a session. Here's all you do.

Tell people that before they can leave the room, they need to have a new idea! It can be any kind of idea at all, as long as they feel it's new. They can close their eyes, daydream, flip through pages of a magazine, play games with whatever odd materials are at hand, or use any other technique they've learned for spurring their creative juices.

As each person comes up with a new idea, he or she should write it down and then raise a hand to be released from the room. The whole process usually takes less than 15 minutes. If some people seem to be stuck, encourage them to carry on!

WHAT D'YA KNOW?

In a Nutshell

Participants take a short quiz that measures their "creativity competencies"–the basic skills that allow people to express creativity. A discussion follows in which people discuss ways of boosting these competencies.

Time

30 minutes.

What You'll Learn

So-called "creative" people have strong creativity competencies–underlying skills and tendencies that allow people to express creativity. These skills can be measured, and we can boost the skills we lack. In other words, everyone has enormous creative potential. To realize that potential, one must strengthen certain key skills: the "core competencies" of creativity.

What You'll Need

Copies of handouts on pages 216 and 217 should be distributed.

What to Do

Distribute copies of the handout on page 216, answer questions people might have about the test, and have people complete it. This should take between 5 and 10 minutes. Then distribute copies of page 217 and have people self-score the tests. The latter will allow people to generate an overall score, as well as sub-scores in the four competency categories:

1) Capturing
2) Challenging
3) Broadening
4) Surrounding

Lead a brief discussion about what these categories mean and how participants might get additional training to sharpen their skills.

Discussion Questions

1. Where are your creativity competencies especially strong? Where could you use some improvement?
2. Were you surprised by the results of the quiz? How so?
3. What additional training would you like to have to improve your creativity competencies? How might this help you express your creativity?

If You're Short on Time

Administer the test orally, having people record their answers on a blank sheet of paper, and then talk them through the scoring.

Tips!

The test included here is a shortened version of the *Epstein Creativity Competencies Inventory for Individuals (ECCI-i)*. The full, validated test can be obtained from InnoGen International (1-877-INNOGEN or www.innogen.com). It can be administered online or on a personal computer. A second test, the *Epstein Creativity Competencies Inventory for Managers (ECCI-m)*, measures eight competencies that help managers, teachers, and others to elicit creativity in other people.

Note that since these tests are competency-based, they avoid the labeling problem: There are no right and wrong answers, and the scores do not suggest that someone is "creative" or "dull." Instead the scores suggest types of training that can improve both the frequency and quality of creative expression.

EPSTEIN CREATIVITY COMPETENCIES INVENTORY
for Individuals (ECCI-i) [Abridged]

Please use a pencil to fill in the bubble that best represents your reaction to each statement.

1. I do not have time to think of new ideas.   *Agree* ① ② ③ ④ ⑤ *Disagree*

2. I do not need to record new ideas to help me remember them.   *Agree* ① ② ③ ④ ⑤ *Disagree*

3. I only read books and articles within my area of expertise.   *Agree* ① ② ③ ④ ⑤ *Disagree*

4. Occasionally I like to work on extremely difficult problems.   *Agree* ① ② ③ ④ ⑤ *Disagree*

5. I keep a recording device near me at all times.   *Agree* ① ② ③ ④ ⑤ *Disagree*

6. I enjoy traveling to new places.   *Agree* ① ② ③ ④ ⑤ *Disagree*

7. I like meeting new people.   *Agree* ① ② ③ ④ ⑤ *Disagree*

8. I only like tasks that have a high probability of success.   *Agree* ① ② ③ ④ ⑤ *Disagree*

9. I rarely change the decorations in my work environment.   *Agree* ① ② ③ ④ ⑤ *Disagree*

10. I record my new ideas as soon as they occur to me.   *Agree* ① ② ③ ④ ⑤ *Disagree*

11. I sometimes use my dreams or daydreams to get new ideas.   *Agree* ① ② ③ ④ ⑤ *Disagree*

12. I often read books and articles from areas outside my specialty.   *Agree* ① ② ③ ④ ⑤ *Disagree*

13. I do not share my ideas with others.   *Agree* ① ② ③ ④ ⑤ *Disagree*

14. I subscribe to magazines in a variety of subject areas.   *Agree* ① ② ③ ④ ⑤ *Disagree*

15. I only seek training within my specialty.   *Agree* ① ② ③ ④ ⑤ *Disagree*

16. Daydreaming only wastes my time.   *Agree* ① ② ③ ④ ⑤ *Disagree*

17. I do not like to work on problems that have no solution.   *Agree* ① ② ③ ④ ⑤ *Disagree*

18. There are special places where I go to think.   *Agree* ① ② ③ ④ ⑤ *Disagree*

19. I would never submit an idea through a suggestion system.   *Agree* ① ② ③ ④ ⑤ *Disagree*

20. I am not afraid of failure.   *Agree* ① ② ③ ④ ⑤ *Disagree*

21. I do not need any more colleagues.   *Agree* ① ② ③ ④ ⑤ *Disagree*

22. I enjoy working with the same group of people all the time.   *Agree* ① ② ③ ④ ⑤ *Disagree*

23. I keep a recording device by my bed at night.   *Agree* ① ② ③ ④ ⑤ *Disagree*

Self-Scorer for ECCI-i [Abridged]

To score your test: Generate your total score by listing a _1_ or a _0_ in the blanks in the left-hand column below. Give yourself a _1_ if you filled in a bubble in the shaded areas; otherwise give yourself a _0_. Count up the 1's and fill in your total score at the bottom of the column. The highest possible score is a _23_. If you scored lower than that, you can probably improve your creativity competencies. To focus on specific competencies, complete the four boxes below by circling item numbers for which you received a score of _1_. In each box, count the 1's, and fill in the blank with the total. If you scored below the maximum, you may need to strengthen your skills within that competency area.

1. ① ② ③ ❹ ❺ ___
2. ① ② ③ ❹ ❺ ___
3. ① ② ③ ❹ ❺ ___
4. ❶ ❷ ③ ④ ⑤ ___
5. ❶ ❷ ③ ④ ⑤ ___
6. ❶ ❷ ③ ④ ⑤ ___
7. ❶ ❷ ③ ④ ⑤ ___
8. ① ② ③ ❹ ❺ ___
9. ① ② ③ ❹ ❺ ___
10. ❶ ❷ ③ ④ ⑤ ___
11. ❶ ❷ ③ ④ ⑤ ___
12. ❶ ❷ ③ ④ ⑤ ___
13. ① ② ③ ❹ ❺ ___
14. ❶ ❷ ③ ④ ⑤ ___
15. ① ② ③ ❹ ❺ ___
16. ① ② ③ ❹ ❺ ___
17. ① ② ③ ❹ ❺ ___
18. ❶ ❷ ③ ④ ⑤ ___
19. ① ② ③ ❹ ❺ ___
20. ❶ ❷ ③ ④ ⑤ ___
21. ① ② ③ ❹ ❺ ___
22. ① ② ③ ❹ ❺ ___
23. ❶ ❷ ③ ④ ⑤ ___

TOTAL SCORE: _____ /23

---

1) Preserves new ideas (Capturing). You preserve new ideas as they occur and manage resources and time to aid in this process.

1	2	5	10	11
13	16	18	19	23

Total 1's: ____ / 10

---

2) Seeks challenges (Challenging). You subject yourself to difficult tasks that require performance outside your current level of skill or knowledge.

4   8   17   20

Total 1's: ____ / 4

---

3) Broadens skills and knowledge (Broadening). You seek training, experience, and knowledge outside your current areas of expertise.

3   12   15

Total 1's: ____ / 3

---

4) Changes physical and social environment (Surrounding). You change your physical and social environment on a regular basis.

6   7   9   14   21   22

Total 1's: ____ / 6

217

INDEX

220

ABOUT THE AUTHOR

One of the world's leading experts on human behavior, ROBERT EPSTEIN is Editor-in-Chief of *Psychology Today* magazine and host of the magazine's nationally syndicated radio program. Dr. Epstein is also University Research Professor at United States International University in San Diego, Chairman and CEO of InnoGen International, and Director Emeritus of the Cambridge Center for Behavioral Studies in Massachusetts. He received his Ph.D. in psychology in 1981 from Harvard University. He is the developer of Generativity Theory, a scientific theory of the creative process, and a contributor to the *Encyclopedia of Creativity*. His research on creativity and problem solving has been reported in *Time* magazine, the *New York Times*, and *Discover*, as well as on national and international radio and television. Epstein's recent books include *The Big Book of Stress-Relief Games* (McGraw-Hill), *Stress-Management and Relaxation Activities for Trainers* (McGraw-Hill), *The New Psychology Today Reader* (Kendall/Hunt), *Creativity Games for Trainers* (McGraw-Hill), *Cognition, Creativity, and Behavior: Selected Essays* (Praeger), *Pure Fitness: Body Meets Mind* (Masters Press, with Lori "Ice" Fetrick of "The American Gladiators"), *Self-Help Without the Hype* (Performance Management Publications), and *Irrelativity* (Astrion). He is also the editor of two books of writings by the eminent psychologist, B. F. Skinner, with whom Epstein collaborated at Harvard. He has served on the faculties of Boston University, the University of Massachusetts at Amherst, the University of California San Diego, and other universities. He served as Professor of Psychology and Chair of the Department of Psychology at National University and was also appointed Research Professor there. He is also Adjunct Professor of Psychology at San Diego State University. Dr. Epstein directed the Loebner Prize Competition in Artificial Intelligence for five years and has done consulting and training for businesses and mental health programs for more than fifteen years. He has been a commentator for NPR's "Marketplace" and the Voice of America, and his popular writings have appeared in *Reader's Digest*, *The Washington Post*, *Psychology Today*, *Good Housekeeping*, *Parenting*, and other magazines and newspapers. Dr. Epstein can be reached by email at repstein@post.harvard.edu.